## INTERACTIVE MANUAL

# UNLOCKING DESTINIES
## FROM THE
# COURTS OF
# HEAVEN

# UNLOCKING DESTINIES
## FROM THE
# COURTS OF
# HEAVEN

### DISSOLVING CURSES THAT
### DELAY AND DENY OUR FUTURES

# ROBERT
# HENDERSON

DESTINY IMAGE® PUBLISHERS, INC.

P.O. Box 310, Shippensburg, PA 17257-0310

*"Promoting Inspired Lives."*

This book and all other Destiny Image and Destiny Image Fiction books are available at Christian bookstores and distributors worldwide.

Cover design by Eileen Rockwell
Interior design by Terry Clifton

For more information on foreign distributors, call 717-532-3040.

Reach us on the Internet: www.destinyimage.com.

ISBN 13 TP: 978-0-7684-1378-6

For Worldwide Distribution, Printed in the U.S.A.

3 4 5 6 7 8 / 21 20 19 18 17

# CONTENTS

# INTRODUCTION

This interactive manual is designed to help you identify and dissolve the delaying forces that prevent you from discovering and walking in the fullness of your destiny. The most common delaying, hindering force aimed at your destiny is a curse.

The desire to see your destiny fulfilled is not a selfish ambition. When the body of Christ starts to see personal destinies fulfilled, by default, the powers of darkness will be pushed back and restrained in the earth. The devil's agenda for individuals, families, regions, and nations will be broken as you step into the assignments God has marked for your life—even before the foundation of the earth.

Throughout this course, you will recognize and confront different hindrances to you walking in the fullness of your destiny. It all begins with approaching God the Judge in the courts of Heaven. Remember, He wants to render judgments on *your* behalf. The key is coming with humility into the courts of Heaven and learning how to navigate this supernatural dimension of prayer.

You can approach this course as follows:

1. You will learn how to interact with God the Judge through courtroom prayer.

2. You will receive a basic understanding of how to operate in the courts of Heaven.

3. You will discover what the books of Heaven or books of destiny are and why they are vital to you fulfilling your purpose.

4. You will evaluate the status of your own destiny: do you have a sense of destiny, but it remains elusive? Do you have no sense of destiny or purpose at all?

5. You will retrieve your book of destiny in Heaven, if it has been sold out.

6. You will open your book of destiny once it has been retrieved.

7. When you have access to your book of destiny, you will be able to have clarity on your purpose and also present cases before the courts of Heaven based on what's written in your book.

8. You will identify several common landing places that have given the devil legal right to plant curses in your life.

9. You will specifically renounce these landing places of legal right and repent for them, cancelling the curses from continuing in your life and in the lives of future generations.

10. You will ask the Lord to give you prophetic sight so that you can begin to discern how the spirit realm operates and thereby freely have access to what is written in the books of destiny in Heaven.

The end goal is:

- Providing you a supernatural prayer strategy where you can begin to prophetically see what is recorded in your unique book of destiny in Heaven.

- Pray these realities into being over your life and family.

- Discern and pray forth what is written in the books of other people, regions, cities, and even nations, as the Holy Spirit reveals.

# HOW TO USE THE INTERACTIVE MANUAL

To get the most out of this experience, it is strongly recommended that you work through this manual and its interactive exercises in conjunction with the *Unlocking Destinies from the Courts of Heaven* curriculum resources. The curriculum can be done as a small group, a class, or an individual experience.

You would first watch the video sessions and then work through the appropriate manual exercises throughout the week. The schedule would involve you working through one session and its interactive exercises each week.

Remember, this resource is for you. Interact with it honestly. Fill up the blank pages and journal space with your thoughts and interactions with the Holy Spirit. It is not intended to simply provide you with information—it is being presented to you as a vehicle to help you unlock your destiny from the courts of Heaven.

If you desire a more exhaustive teaching on the topic of dissolving curses and dealing with delaying forces to your destiny, it is recommended that you watch the curriculum video sessions and read through the books *Operating in the Courts of Heaven* and *Unlocking Destinies from the Courts of Heaven*.

## SUMMARY

You will receive an introductory summary of each session.

## INTERACTIVE DISCUSSION QUESTIONS

You can answer these discussion questions individually by writing in the space provided or in a small group/Bible study class through oral discussion and conversation. If you go through the sessions with a group or class, it is still recommended that you personally work through each of the interactive discussion questions on your own time so you can fully process the concepts you are learning.

## ACTIVATION EXERCISES

These exercise can be done in a group setting or by an individual.

If the activation segment is being done in a group or class setting, it is recommended that the group leader takes an appropriate amount of time at the end of the class time and sets it aside for both the activation segment and questions/answers from those who want to share about their experience during the segment. This is where the information learned in the sessions will be processed and implemented.

# DEVOTIONAL READINGS

These entries are intended to help reinforce the concepts you learned about while watching the video sessions—although they can be read and interacted with outside of watching the sessions.

# Session 1

# THREE DIMENSIONS OF PRAYER: FATHER, FRIEND, AND JUDGE

*It could be that unanswered prayers have nothing to do with the timing of God. It could be that a legal matter is causing resistance against us in the spirit realm; a legal issue is stopping God from answering our prayers.*

Session 1 begins with the most important foundation for unlocking destinies from the courts of Heaven—recognizing the three dimensions of prayer. We know our Lord as our heavenly Father, and we know He is our Best Friend, but how well do you know Him as the Judge? By the time you finish this course, you will know Him intimately as the Judge—and how and why to approach Him in that capacity.

First, let's discuss the importance of prayer. Jesus taught about prayer throughout the Gospels. In Matthew and Mark, for instance, Jesus illustrates prayer in a variety of ways. At times, He would pray all night long, He would get up very early in the morning to pray, or He would go off by Himself to pray. In the book of John, principles of prayer are cited. But in the book of Luke in particular, Jesus painted word pictures of prayer so we would understand what was going on in the spirit realm when we pray.

One of the main shifts for me when I began to understand the courts of Heaven was my concept of the spirit realm. I used to think that the spirit realm was a battlefield. When I discovered that the conflict in the spirit realm is actually in the courtroom, I was surprised at first. It's true that in the spirit realm, we are in a conflict when we pray. But here's the issue—*where* is that conflict being played out? Conflict on a battlefield and conflict in a courtroom are two separate things. If I'm in a courtroom but I think I'm on a battlefield, I could be using the wrong protocol to accomplish the goal.

When people have been praying prayers for a long time and haven't seen an answer, they may think, *I must be doing something wrong. I must be displeasing to God. Maybe I don't have enough faith.* We start blaming unanswered prayer on ourselves or think that it's not the timing of God. All the while, life is falling apart. Marriages are being destroyed. There is financial ruin. People are dying prematurely, and yet many chalk it up to the timing of God. I think it's a crazy idea to think that evil, even irreversible bad things happen because it's not the time of God to answer my prayer.

It could be that it has nothing to do with the timing of God. It could be that a legal matter is causing resistance against us in the spirit realm; a legal issue is stopping God from answering our prayers.

To understand that premise, it is important to study the three dimensions of prayer Jesus taught in Luke 11 and Luke 18. The disciples came to Jesus in Luke 11:1-2 and asked Him, *"Lord, teach us to pray."* Day after day they were watching Him pray and wanted His advice. In response to their request, Jesus said, *"When you pray, say: 'Our Father in heaven, hallowed be Your name.'"*

His discussion of prayer certainly included the identity of God as *Father*, but it did not end there. In this session, you will discover how three different identities of God actually involve three different prayer strategies!

## SUMMARY

To pray effectively, it's important to recognize how to interact with the One you are praying to—God. He is a Person, not a formula. As a result, believers must learn how to relate to the different personality expressions of God when it comes to interacting with Him in prayer.

In the Gospels, Jesus offers three dimensions of prayer by introducing us to three unique identities of God—each one corresponding to a different posture in prayer. He is identified as Father, Friend, and Judge.

This first session is an introduction to the foundational concept of operating in the courts of Heaven—recognizing God as Judge. You will better understand the distinct prayer approaches that you can take based on what personality of God you are relating to.

> **YOU MIGHT BE SEEING DELAY IN PRAYER BECAUSE SOMETHING *LEGAL* IS RESISTING YOU IN THE SPIRIT REALM.**

## INTERACTIVE QUESTIONS

1. Explain why you might be experiencing resistance or delay in prayer? List some possible reasons.

2. Read Luke 11:1-2. Explain how you would approach God the *Father* in the place of prayer.

   *"Lord, teach us to pray, as John also taught his disciples." So He said to them, "When you pray, say: Our Father in heaven, hallowed be Your name. Your kingdom come" (Luke 11:1-2).*

3. What do the names *Abba* and *Father* reveal about the nature of God the Father? How are they unique?

   - Abba:

   - Father:

> **IF WE ONLY KNOW GOD AS ABBA, THAT WILL LEAD TO *LAWLESSNESS*. IF WE ONLY KNOW GOD AS FATHER, THAT WILL LEAD TO *LEGALISM*.**

4. Read Luke 11:5–8.

*And He said to them, "Which of you shall have a friend, and go to him at midnight and say to him, 'Friend, lend me three loaves; for a friend of mine has come to me on his journey, and I have nothing to set before him'; and he will answer from within and say, 'Do not trouble me; the door is now shut, and my children are with me in bed; I cannot rise and give to you'? I say to you, though he will not rise and give to him because he is his friend, yet because of his persistence he will rise and give him as many as he needs* (Luke 11:5–8).

When you approach God as *Friend*, describe what posture you are taking in the place of prayer.

_____

_____

_____

_____

_____

_____

5. List some examples of friends of God in the Old Testament. How did these individuals specifically relate to God?

_____

_____

_____

_____

_____

_____

_____

---

### FRIENDS ARE THOSE GOD CAN SHARE HIS *SECRETS* WITH.

---

6. When approach God as an intercessor, what is your prayer assignment? Explain how you think you should be praying.

 

7. Discuss the following statement and its implications: "If judgment comes to a nation, it's because the government of God failed in its assignment."

   How is the assignment of the people of God directly connected to the future and destiny of nations?

 

8. Read Luke 18:1–8.

   This reveals a picture of God as Judge.

   > *Then He spoke a parable to them, that men always ought to pray and not lose heart, saying: "There was in a certain city a judge who did not fear God nor regard man. Now there was a widow in that city; and she came to him, saying, 'Get justice for me from my adversary.' And he would not for a while; but afterward he said within himself, 'Though I do not fear God*

*nor regard man, yet because this widow troubles me I will avenge her, lest by her continual coming she weary me.'"*

*Then the Lord said, "Hear what the unjust judge said. And shall God not avenge His own elect who cry out day and night to Him, though He bears long with them? I tell you that He will avenge them speedily"* (Luke 18:1–8).

At this point, discuss what each of the identities of God that Jesus introduces reveals about how you approach God in prayer.

- Father: Luke 11:1-2

- Friend: Luke 11:5–8

- Judge: Luke 18:1–9

9.  Why/when would you approach God as Judge?

# ACTIVATION EXERCISE

Following this session, take some time to interact with God in prayer. It is essential that these sessions provide a spiritual laboratory where you can actually experiment with these new concepts.

1.  Make a list of prayer requests. If you are in a group setting, encourage each person to make a list of the different things they are praying for themselves, for others, etc. *Space is provided for you in this interactive manual to write down your current list of Prayer Needs.*

2.  After a few minutes, break up the prayer requests into categories based on the Father, Friend, Judge model. Space is provided where you can list different prayer needs under the three identities of God—Father, Friend, and Judge.

The goal is learning how different requests call for different prayer strategies. Based on what you learned about relating with God your Father, God your Friend, and God your Judge, categorize your prayer requests.

Most likely, you will be most comfortable with identifying your personal needs (God the Father) and needs of others (God your Friend). In future sessions, you will receive greater clarity on interacting with God the Judge, as this is where the courts of Heaven strategy will come into effect.

# PRAYER NEEDS LIST

# PRAYERS FOR PERSONAL NEEDS

## GOD YOUR FATHER

# PRAYERS FOR OTHERS/INTERCESSION

## GOD YOUR FRIEND

# Prayers Dealing with the Adversary

## God Your Judge

# THE FIRST DIMENSION OF PRAYER: GOD AS FATHER

*For your Father knows the things you have need of before you ask Him. In this manner, therefore, pray: Our Father in heaven, hallowed be Your name.*
—MATTHEW 6:8-9

According to the beginning of the Lord's Prayer in Matthew 6, Jesus indicates that the first dimension of prayer is approaching God as *Father*. Sadly, many believers do not have a right concept of God as Father because of an unfortunate earthly father experience.

Thankfully, though, in Romans 8:15 Paul tells us that we have received the *"Spirit of adoption"* so we can cry out to God, *"Abba, Father."* Only by the Spirit of adoption can we know Him as Father. So often we emphasize the Abba, but forget the Father. Paul was not repeating himself when he said the Spirit would create a cry of "Abba, Father." He was acknowledging that the fatherhood of God has two aspects—the Abba side, which is loving, endearing, always accepting. He'll never reject you, will heal you, will do all the things you desire and need to be done for His will to be fulfilled in our lives. But He also has a Father side, the authority side.

My wife, Mary, and I have raised six children, and there were times when I had to stop being abba and be father to our children. If there was going to be order in our home, I had to be father. I had to draw boundaries and provide discipline and do all the things necessary for order in our home—so they could be prepared for their destiny.

We have to know God in both dimensions, Abba Father—both the endearing, loving, accepting, non-rejecting God He is and the Father who will discipline us for our own good so we can become partakers of His holiness.

Paul says that when the Spirit of adoption comes, we will experience both aspects of the fatherhood of God. Why do I believe this? Because Jesus says the first dimension of prayer is to approach God as Father. So whenever I approach Him, I approach Him as Abba Father, the One who loves me unconditionally, but also the One who will prepare me for my future and the destiny that He has for me—anything less as a Father would be irresponsible. He loves me enough to prepare and to correct me when I need to be corrected and to deal with me about issues that need to be dealt with—my marriage, raising my children, improving my character, or whatever it may have been, God says, "I'm going to work in you My very nature, so you cannot only reflect Me but you also know Me, not just as Abba and not just as Father, but as Abba Father."

Knowing Him only as Abba leads to lawlessness. Because He's all-accepting and loving, my flesh tends to take advantage of that generosity. Does yours? Mine does. So I need to know Him as Abba, I need that aspect of who He is. But if that's all I know of Him, I will become lawless in my nature and my activities.

On the other hand, if I only know Him as Father, the One who has authority, then I will become a legalist. I'll try my best to please Him because of His authority. And guess what? Lawlessness and legalism mingle at the same place—death.

God says He's going to come to us and by His Spirit will reveal Abba Father, the One who is all-accepting but also the One who will prepare you for your God-given destiny and future—one that is wonderful and beyond your comprehension.

I believe we have to be firmly established in approaching God as Father, because that is the basis for every other thing we do. I believe with every fiber of my being that when we approach Him as Father God, as the loving heavenly Father, as Abba Father, He will reveal Himself to us in those roles.

## BIBLE STUDY

Read Matthew 6:8-9, Romans 8:15.

Explain your understanding of God as *Father* and how you would specifically relate to Him in this role through prayer?

Father - A more mature Relationship, provider.
protector, Teacher, one that Listens, helps
make decisions, gives guidance

# THE SECOND DIMENSION OF PRAYER: GOD AS FRIEND

*And He said to them, "Which of you shall have a friend, and go to him at midnight and say to him, 'Friend, lend me three loaves; for a friend of mine has come to me on his journey, and I have nothing to set before him'; and he will answer from within and say, 'Do not trouble me; the door is now shut, and my children are with me in bed; I cannot rise and give to you'? I say to you, though he will not rise and give to him because he is his friend, yet because of his persistence he will rise and give him as many as he needs.*
—LUKE 11:5–8

In Luke 11:5–8, Jesus unveils another way we approach God, which is the second dimension of prayer. He tells the story of friend A who comes knocking at friend B's door at midnight and asks for bread to feed friend C who had stopped by on a journey. Friend A asks friend B to please get out of bed and give him what he needs so he can help friend C. Even though friend B doesn't want to get up, he will and he will give friend A what he wants. (My version is that he gets up and gives him the bread so he would leave him alone and he can go back to sleep.) That's the basis of the parable.

First Jesus teaches about approaching God as Father, which is the basis of all praying and all relationship with God. And the second dimension is approaching Him as Friend. We can know Him as Father without knowing Him as Friend.

What makes God our Friend? Jesus says in John 15:15, *"No longer do I call you servants…but I have called you friends, for all things that I heard from My Father I have made known to you."* God can share His secrets with His friends. Sometimes a father can't, and shouldn't, share everything with his children. But friends can be trusted with secrets and truths.

Why is it important to approach God as your Friend? Well, we don't have to look any further than Abraham for a good example. Abraham was called the Friend of God multiple times in Scripture. As a friend, God confided in Abraham about what He was going to do about Sodom and Gomorrah (see Gen. 18:20-21). God told Abraham He was going to destroy the city because its evilness demanded His justice. Why did God tell Abraham beforehand? Maybe He wanted Abraham to give Him a reason not to destroy the city and its citizens. Why? Because *God is always looking for a reason to be merciful.*

When we understand that quality of God, we will quit condemning what God's not condemning. We will quit judging what God is not judging. Jesus said we condemn the guiltless because we don't understand—He desires mercy, not sacrifice.

God tells Abraham about destroying Sodom and Gomorrah for one reason—Abraham as His friend knows His heart. Abraham as the friend of God knew the heart of God and knew the secrets of God, so Abraham knew God was telling him about the disaster because He wanted Abraham to do something about it.

## BIBLE STUDY

Read Luke 11:5–8, John 15:15, Genesis 18:16–33.

Explain your understanding of God as *Friend* and how you would specifically relate to Him in this role through prayer?

Use Genesis 18:16–33 as an example, where Abraham intercedes for Sodom and Gomorrah. Explain how Abraham was approaching God as Friend.

# INTERCEDING AS A FRIEND OF GOD

*And the Scripture was fulfilled which says, "Abraham believed God, and it was accounted to him for righteousness." And he was called the friend of God.*
—JAMES 2:23

*So the Lord spoke to Moses face to face, as a man speaks to his friend.*
—EXODUS 33:11

*No longer do I call you servants, for a servant does not know what his master is doing; but I have called you friends, for all things that I heard from My Father I have made known to you.*
—JOHN 15:15

Many times in my life I have known things on a national level about the United States of America—only because God told me about them. At the time, I would think, *Why is He telling me this? Why am I seeing this? Why am I knowing this? I have no platform to do anything about it.* It seemed that God wanted me to step before Him as His friend and give Him reasons to stop or change what was going to happen.

For instance, in 2008 in the US, before the stock market crashed and the housing industry imploded, I saw the Dow Jones in a dream in the form of a gauge. I saw the indicator drop within the gauge with such force. In the dream, there was a line on the gauge, and I knew if the indicator dropped below that line, the economic structure was going to be destroyed and would not recover. Although it came close, I also knew that it had not gone past that line. Three things were clear to me: 1) the horror associated with a fall; 2) it would recover; and 3) those who were rightly positioned would make a lot of money when it did recover.

Because I knew all that to be true, I went to some of the people who had much bigger platforms than I had and told them what I saw in the dream. They laughed at me. *Robert thinks the stock market is going to crash—ha!* So I just laughed it off too, but it wasn't long before what I said happened exactly.

I realize now that God wanted me as His friend, and probably many others, to come before Him and say, "Lord, is there anything we can do about this so the destruction that's going to come to earth won't happen or it won't have to be as bad?" This is what the *ecclesia* (a united Church that extends beyond the earthly realm into Heaven) is called to do. We are called to be His friend.

I thank God for meeting our own personal needs, but God has a governmental place in the spirit realm that He wants us to take that can shift the nations of the earth in significant ways concerning commerce, conflicts, etc. How do I know this? Because Hebrews 12:23 says, *"to the church of the firstborn, whose names are written in heaven"* (NIV). In other words, if we know how to move into this realm, we can make significant impact in positive ways for the Kingdom. That's exactly what Abraham was doing. He was dealing with an issue concerning a region of the earth.

# BIBLE STUDY

Read James 2:23, Exodus 33:11 and John 15:15.

Reflect on the roles of intercession that both Moses and Abraham had as friends of God. Explain what it would look like for you to model their friendship with God through *your* intercession?

If God was to reveal something negative to you (in a dream, vision, word, etc.), how should you respond in the place of intercession?

# THE THIRD DIMENSION OF PRAYER: GOD AS JUDGE

*Then He spoke a parable to them, that men always ought to pray and not lose heart,*
*saying: "There was in a certain city a judge who did not fear God nor regard man. Now*
*there was a widow in that city; and she came to him, saying, 'Get justice for me from my*
*adversary.' And he would not for a while; but afterward he said within himself, 'Though*
*I do not fear God nor regard man, yet because this widow troubles me I will avenge*
*her, lest by her continual coming she weary me.'" Then the Lord said, "Hear what the*
*unjust judge said. And shall God not avenge His own elect who cry out day and night*
*to Him, though He bears long with them? I tell you that He will avenge them speedily.*
*Nevertheless, when the Son of Man comes, will He really find faith on the earth?"*
—LUKE 18:1–8

In Luke 18:1 (NIV), Jesus says, *"Then Jesus told his disciples a parable to show them that they should always pray and not give up* [not lose heart]." His purpose for this teaching is to make them aware of another dimension of prayer that will give them answers the other realms didn't. Jesus is saying in essence, "I'm about to give you a secret that will bring breakthrough. The other two dimensions are great, but any prayers not answered there will be answered in the third dimension—approaching God as Judge."

Consider what Jesus shared in Luke 18:1–8, a parable about persistence.

The unjust judge would not give the woman justice *"for a while."* Why would he? He's unjust. He doesn't render verdicts on the basis of justice, he renders verdicts based on what he can get out of it—a bribe, promotion, fame, whatever the situation. Jesus says the widow has nothing—no influence, no money to bribe the judge, so he doesn't give her the justice she seeks right away.

But the judge's problem was that the widow kept coming back. Every time the judge turned around, she was back on the docket. That's the way judges are approached in the courtroom. A person cannot knock on a judge's door at home. Judges can only be approached in a judicial system. So this judge finally says he's going to give the widow what she wants. He's going to avenge her of her adversary and give her justice—because he's weary of continually seeing and hearing her.

Jesus says that God will avenge His people who cry out to Him day and night. He will reward them quickly. If you learn how to come into the judicial system, your answers will come speedily. Why? Because something legal is preventing your prayers from being answered. Approaching God as Father hasn't worked and approaching Him as Friend hasn't worked, but knowing how to approach God as Judge will bring swift answers. Step into the judicial system of Heaven and you will see a shift legally in the spirit.

The moral of the persistent woman's story is not that God is an unjust judge whom you have to convince and then wait for an undetermined time for a ruling. The truth of the story is that if the widow could get a ruling from an unjust judge, we can get a speedy ruling when we come before the God and Righteous Judge of all the universe because we are His elect.

## BIBLE STUDY

Reflect on Luke 18:1–8.

How does this parable connect the identity of God as *Judge* with a prayer strategy that will bring *breakthrough*?

_____

_____

_____

_____

_____

_____

_____

_____

_____

_____

_____

_____

_____

_____

_____

_____

# CONFRONTING YOUR ADVERSARY

*Then He spoke a parable to them, that men always ought to pray and not lose heart, saying: "There was in a certain city a judge who did not fear God nor regard man. Now there was a widow in that city; and she came to him, saying, 'Get justice for me from my adversary.'"*
—LUKE 18:1-3

When we approach God as Judge when we're dealing with an adversary, we are acknowledging that there may be a legal case against us.

When referring to prayer, Jesus didn't cite a battlefield; He put it in a courtroom setting. Paul talks about battlefields in different situations, but Jesus didn't equate prayer with a battlefield.

In Revelation 19:11, the Bible says that when Jesus comes back on the white horse with the armies of Heaven with Him, He will come to judge, which is judicial activity, and then to make war. Here's the point. You'll never go to war against your adversary until you've first been to court.

If you try to go to war against your adversary before you've been to court, there will be backlash. The enemy can only bring a case against you if he has the legal right to present it. There's an order in the spirit realm that we need to make sure we're walking in accordance with, so we are functionally operating from the rank and the position from which God wants us to operate.

The word *adversary* in Luke 18:3—*"Get justice for me from my adversary"*—is the Greek word *antidikos,* and it means one who brings a lawsuit. It's a legal position in the spirit realm. The same word is cited in 1 Peter 5:8—*"Be sober, be vigilant, because your adversary the devil…."* The devil is occupying a legal position. He has the right to bring lawsuits. Because the devil is always trying to gang up on us, Peter says we must be sober and vigilant, ensuring we do not give him any right to build a case against us legally. The devil cannot devour us at will. He has to discover a legal right to do so. If he could devour at will, we'd all be dead. But he can't. He can only devour when he has found a legal right.

This is why you've been praying prayers for years that are in agreement with God's Word, yet there's been no answer. The enemy has a legal right to deny what's rightfully yours. He has a case against you in the spirit realm—that you will never deal with by approaching God as Father. You will never deal with it approaching God as Friend. You have to deal with it by going before Him as Judge and stepping into the judicial system of Heaven and undoing the case of the *antidikos* against you. The moment God dismisses the adversary's case against you, the answer comes quickly.

Father is great. Friend is wonderful. Both of these prayer approaches have a much-needed place in the life of every believer. But going before the Judge gets breakthrough answers.

## BIBLE STUDY

Read 1 Peter 5:8 in conjunction with Luke 18:1–8.

How does approaching God as Judge specifically deal with your adversary, the devil?

Roman 8:2 - Law of the spirit of life in Christ Jesus has set me free from the law of sin and Death
2 laws - Law of sin and death
Law of the spirit of life in Christ Jesus

# Session 2

# OPERATING IN THE COURTS OF HEAVEN

*It takes courtroom operation and courtroom activity to
be able to reach the destiny God has for you.*

Session 1 presented the foundational understanding of the three dimensions of prayer and how to move from not just seeking God as Father, not just as Friend, but also approaching Him as Judge in the judicial system of Heaven.

I've discovered that the ability to approach Him as Judge is critically important for breakthrough. God has for *every person* a destiny that's been prepared before the foundations of the earth, but here's the thing—it takes courtroom operation and courtroom activity to be able to reach the destiny God has for you.

Everywhere I go I hear frustration in the voices of God's people because they sense they were created and designed for something more than what they are currently. If you are shaking your head yes after reading that statement, that's normal. Most everyone thinks they could or should be accomplishing more. Maybe you're thinking, *I'm supposed to be having a greater impact at home, at church, at work....*

I have found that the key to "more" is to know how to go into the courts of Heaven and remove every legal thing in the spirit that the enemy is using to prevent you from becoming and accomplishing what God made you for. God is not resisting you. The enemy is blocking you from coming into the fullness of what God had in mind when He created you.

# SUMMARY

Now that you have a basic understanding of the three postures of prayer—based on the three identities of God described by Jesus—you can focus more on the courtroom activity of Heaven, which involves God as the Righteous Judge.

When it comes to this courtroom language, many believers actually draw back in fear as the identity of God as Judge projects images of Judgment Day, condemnation, and guilt. The hesitancy Christians have in approaching God as Judge is due to a calculated effort of the enemy to undermine this essential identity of the Lord.

As a result, the adversary has done what he can to tarnish it because he fears you assuming this posture in prayer as it directly targets and dismantles his activity. Even though there will be a Judgment Day, the identity of God as Judge speaks of One who wishes to render verdicts on our behalf. This is the picture we must paint for ourselves if we are going to successfully operate in the courts of Heaven and dissolve curses that the adversary uses to detour and prevent destinies from coming to pass.

> **IN EVERY PICTURE JESUS PAINTED OF PRAYER,**
> **HE NEVER PUT PRAYER ONTO A BATTLEFIELD,**
> **BUT HE DID PUT IT INTO A COURTROOM.**

# INTERACTIVE QUESTIONS

1. Explain the essential difference between the "battlefield" and "courtroom" postures in prayer. How can the battlefield approach actually be counterproductive?

2. Read 1 Peter 5:8.

   *Be sober, be vigilant; because your adversary the devil walks about like a roaring lion, seeking whom he may devour* (1 Peter 5:8).

   Describe your understanding of how the devil, your adversary, devours people?

   _____

   _____

   _____

   _____

   _____

   _____

   _____

   _____

3. Explain how *sin* gives the devil legal right in your life. (Read and review Psalm 32 and Psalm 51.)

   _____

   _____

   _____

   _____

   _____

   _____

   _____

   _____

   _____

4. Explain what *transgression* is and how it can give the devil legal right in your life.

   _____

   _____

   _____

   _____

   _____

5.  Explain your understanding of *iniquity* and how the devil can use iniquity to enter into your life—and even future generations.

_____

_____

_____

_____

_____

_____

_____

6.  How does iniquity give the devil a legal right to tempt you in a specific area?

_____

_____

_____

_____

_____

_____

_____

_____

_____

**ALMOST ALL *STRONGHOLDS* COME
FROM AN INIQUITOUS ROOT.**

7.  What impact can iniquity have on your identity—the way you think about yourself?

_____

8. How can *not* dealing with iniquity prevent you from walking into your destiny?

9. How does the enemy use iniquity to try and build cases against you?

10. Explain how iniquity can actually be standing in the way of seeing prayers answered.

# ACTIVATION EXERCISE

For this particular session, the activation is a very personal process that involves you prayerfully asking the Lord to reveal any sin, transgression, or iniquity that might be in your life.

Please know, the process of dealing with these issues should not be lengthy or drawn out. It's not works-based. It does not have to take several months, weeks, or even hours. The reason believers live with these issues destroying their lives is simply because they never resolve to confront them and deal with them.

In the following pages, it is recommended that you go through the following interactive process so you can identify areas of sin, transgression, and iniquity; pray through it; renounce it; and position yourself to step into your destiny in new dimensions that, perhaps, you have never experienced.

Remember, the devil is a legalist, and he is looking to use anything against you to restrain you from fulfilling your God-ordained purpose.

1. **Pray and ask the Holy Spirit to lead you into all truth.** Do *not* become introspective—intentionally trying to find everything wrong with your life through this process. This is the counterfeit of genuine conviction.

   God is a loving Father who takes us from glory to glory. If He were to reveal every single area of our lives that needed adjustment all at once, we would be overwhelmed and feel defeated. The adversary will attempt to try and move you in this direction, so be vigilant and on guard during this process.

   - **Condemnation** comes from the devil and will always leave you feeling overwhelmed, overcome, and disempowered. The fruit of condemnation is hopelessness.

   - **Conviction** comes from the Spirit of God and is accompanied by the hope of victory. While the Holy Spirit will reveal to you areas of your life that are under the influence of darkness, He will come with the power and strategy to give you victory, thus filling you with hope.

2. **Ask the Lord to open the courts of Heaven for you.** We do not demand or command this—this is a privilege that God the Judge extends to us out of His mercy.

3. Now, ask the Holy Spirit to shine His light of conviction onto the following areas:

   a. **Sin:** areas where you have missed the mark.

   b. **Transgression:** areas where you stepped across a line; activity against God.

   c. **Iniquity:** sin that is in the bloodline.

4. For **sin and transgression**, simply repent for these things. Rather than providing a comprehensive list here, ask the Holy Spirit to convict you of these items so you can repent of them, turn away from these snares of the enemy, and take further steps toward fulfilling your destiny.

   a.   Repent for areas where you have missed the mark of the Lord.

   b.   Repent for areas where you did the right things for the *wrong reasons*.

   c.   Repent for impure motives and thoughts.

   d.   Repent for actions and deeds that are contrary to the will of God.

5. For **iniquity**—which is sin in the bloodline—you will need to deal with this slightly differently. In a future session, you will receive instruction on how to break and dissolve curses that have landed upon you and are hijacking your destiny.

   For right now, ask the Holy Spirit to start making these bloodline sins known to you. And remember, refuse to allow condemnation or fear to enter into this process. This is a sign that the enemy is trying to interfere because he is threatened by your freedom.

# SESSION NOTES

# UNDERSTANDING THE COURTS OF HEAVEN

*I watched till thrones were put in place, and the Ancient of Days was seated; His garment was white as snow, and the hair of His head was like pure wool. His throne was a fiery flame, its wheels a burning fire; a fiery stream issued and came forth from before Him. A thousand thousands ministered to Him; ten thousand times ten thousand stood before Him. The court was seated, and the books were opened.*
—**DANIEL 7:9-10**

Daniel 7:10 is the best Scripture verse describing the courts of Heaven. There was activity around the throne; the court of Heaven is there; there is a literal court. And even though in the natural our feet are planted here on planet earth, in the spirit the Bible says *we're seated together with Him in heavenly places* (see Eph. 2:6). We literally are part, a necessary part, of the operation of the courts of Heaven. The courts of Heaven cannot render the verdicts that God desires without our activity there. And so the Bible says that the court was seated—it came to order, was ready to function, ready to render verdicts—and the books were opened.

Daniel 7:25 says:

> He [the anti-Christ or the anti-Christ spirit] shall speak pompous words against the Most High, shall persecute the saints of the Most High, and shall intend to change times and law. Then the saints shall be given into his hand for a time and times and half a time.

Regardless what we may ask or think eschatology-wise, this verse refers to the anti-Christ or the anti-Christ spirit that is persecuting the saints. Although the last portion of the verse says that *the saints will be given over into his hands,* the next two verses reveal:

> But the court shall be seated, and they [the court, the activity of the court, notice "they" not just God, but "they"] shall take away his [anti-Christ's] dominion, to consume and destroy it forever. Then the kingdom and dominion, and the greatness of the kingdoms under the whole heaven, shall be given to the people, the saints of the Most High. His kingdom is an everlasting kingdom, and all dominions shall serve and obey Him (Daniel 7:26-27).

Although the saints—you and I—might be in an absolutely defeated place, one verdict from the court brings them—us—out of defeat and into dominion. One verdict rendered from the seated court took them from a place of total defeat, where everything was ruling over them, into a place of absolute dominion. It took only one verdict, one rendering from the court.

When we go into the courts of Heaven, we can learn to function there as part of the court; the Bible tells us that Jesus has given us that place by virtue of what He did for us. We can approach God not only as Father and Friend, but actually approach Him as Judge in His judicial system. We can see things shift and move from defeat to dominion!

---

**ONE VERDICT FROM THE COURT CAN BRING
YOU OUT OF DEFEAT AND INTO DOMINION.**

---

## BIBLE STUDY

Read Daniel 7:9-10.

Explain how a verdict from the courts of Heaven can bring you out of defeat into dominion. How is a verdict from the courts important to your breakthrough?

_____

_____

_____

_____

_____

_____

_____

_____

_____

_____

_____

_____

# YOUR ADVERSARY IN THE COURTS OF HEAVEN

*Be sober, be vigilant; because your adversary the devil walks
about like a roaring lion, seeking whom he may devour.*
—1 PETER 5:8

You need to know that the devil doesn't want you to fulfill your destiny or purpose. If he can stop you from fleshing out on the earth what's written about you in Heaven, if he can keep you from your destiny, then he can stop the purpose of God from being done on the earth. The purpose of God on the earth is connected to His people reaching their destiny. If you don't reach your destiny, then the purpose of God doesn't get done and God's will becomes frustrated on the earth.

Then guess what happens? God has to wait for the next generation—because God's will *will* get done. He allowed an entire generation to die off in the wilderness so the next one would fulfill His will. Make no mistake, God's will *will get done.* But the issue is, the enemy can keep postponing the will of God, postponing the purposes of God by keeping us from going after and reaching our destiny. The enemy has a vested interest in stopping our destiny so he can stop the purposes of God and prolong what God really wants to see happen.

In the sessions ahead, you will receive a clearer understanding of *what* the devil is seeking to oppose that's written in your book in Heaven. For right now, you need to recognize that you have an adversary seeking to make a case against you.

God wants us to fulfill the destiny He designed for us. How does the devil stop us? Luke 22:31-32 says that Jesus said to Simon Peter, *"Simon, Simon! Indeed, Satan has asked for you, that he may sift you as wheat. But I have prayed for you, that your faith should not fail."* The devil demanded that Simon be put on trial. Jesus said to Peter, Satan has built a case against you, Peter, and he has demanded the right to bring you into court and put you on trial—because he wants to stop you from getting what's in your book. Satan has an awareness of what is written in your book. How would he have that? Again, I cover that in an upcoming session.

When a person's book of destiny is open, then not only can he or she begin to see the revelation in it, but I believe the spirit realm, both good and bad, can see into the book as well, because it's open. So somehow or another the adversary has an awareness that God wants to use Peter to change the world, to alter history.

Peter, a carnal fisherman, is going to be used by Jesus to alter history. Satan may have thought, *I'm going to stop Peter. But how? How can I keep him from getting what's in his book? I know! I'll build a case against him and demand the right to put him on trial in the courts of Heaven.* Satan desired or demanded Peter be put on trial.

All of us who have a Kingdom purpose also have a case against us in Heaven. This is why you're frustrated.

- Why do I feel like I was made for something more than I have been able to accomplish in my life so far?

- Why do I have this awareness about me? Why do I gravitate toward that?

- What makes me feel this way?

There's a case presented by your adversary against you in Heaven that's stopping you from the ultimate fulfillment of what's been written in the books of Heaven about you. Remember Daniel 7:10? *"The court was seated, and the books were opened."*

There is good news, though: *You have an Advocate named Jesus!* In the following segment, you will discover how Jesus steps in on your behalf. For now, it's important that you recognize the reality of your adversary, as this is your essential first step to victory in the courts of Heaven.

## BIBLE STUDY

Read 1 Peter 5:8.

Peter was well acquainted with the language he was using, citing the devil as our adversary. In the Gospels, Jesus actually rebukes Peter for operating under the devil's influence.

Explain your understanding of how the devil is looking to build a case against you in the court of Heaven and how this is aimed at your destiny.

_____

_____

_____

_____

_____

_____

_____

# HOW THE ADVERSARY BUILDS CASES AGAINST US

*My little children, these things I write to you, so that you may not sin. And if anyone sins, we have an Advocate with the Father, Jesus Christ the righteous. And He Himself is the propitiation for our sins, and not for ours only but also for the whole world.*
—1 JOHN 2:1-2

How does the enemy build a case against us? What are the legalities he uses to stop God from answering prayers? There are three basic accusations that can be used against us. In Psalm 32 and 51, David spoke three distinct words when dealing with unrighteousness before God: *sin, transgression,* and *iniquity.* Today, we will focus specifically on sin and transgression. *Sin* means "to miss the mark" in both Hebrew and Greek. It also has to do with motive. Motive is very important, because in the book of Job chapters 1 and 2 the accuser brought a case against Job on the basis of Job's motives.

God asked the enemy when He was in the courtroom with the enemy, *"Have you considered My servant Job"* (Job 1:8). Do you have a case against him? Satan told God that Job only served Him because He put a hedge about him. If God would take the hedge away, Job wouldn't serve Him. The enemy was saying Job's motives for serving God were wrong. The accusation against Job was his motive and intent of heart. That means not only are we to do the right things, *we are to do the right things for the right reasons.*

Why could the enemy accuse Job on the basis of motive? When Job's children had birthday parties or celebrations, Job would sacrifice a burnt offering to God, saying, *"Perhaps my children have sinned and cursed God in their hearts"* (Job 1:5 NIV). Job's offerings were to manipulate God so that his kids would not suffer judgment from perhaps cursing God in their hearts. His motive wasn't, "I love You, God." His motive was, "I'm going to give You this offering so maybe You'll turn a blind eye to anything my kids have done wrong."

The second legal accusation the enemy uses against us is *transgression*. Transgression means to stride or step across a line. It speaks of activity against God. Whereas *sin* may be more about motive and enmity of the heart, *transgression* is about activity. We need to follow all of God's admonitions and repent quickly. Why? Because we have an adversary, an *antidikos,* looking for a legal right to devour us. I try to abide by 1 John 2:1-2:

> *My little children, these things I write to you, so that you may not sin. And if anyone sins, we have an Advocate with the Father, Jesus Christ the righteous. And He Himself is the propitiation for our sins, and not for ours only but also for the whole world.*

Jesus Christ the Righteous is standing on our behalf before the Judge. We can go into the courts of Heaven and say, "Please, I repent and ask for the life blood of Jesus to speak for me. The blood that speaks better things than that of Abel. May Jesus the Advocate speak for me and all the voices, I'm asking for these things to be done."

# REFLECTION

Describe the difference between *sin* and *transgression*. How can the adversary build cases against people based on both of these?

_____

_____

_____

_____

_____

_____

_____

_____

Explain how a lifestyle of "quick repentance" can protect someone from the adversary's tactics. (Review 1 John 2:1-2.)

_____

_____

_____

_____

_____

_____

# THE CASE OF INIQUITY

*Have mercy upon me, O God, according to Your lovingkindness; according to the multitude of Your tender mercies, blot out my transgressions. Wash me thoroughly from my iniquity, and cleanse me from my sin. For I acknowledge my transgressions, and my sin is always before me. Against You, You only, have I sinned, and done this evil in Your sight—that You may be found just when You speak, and blameless when You judge. Behold, I was brought forth in iniquity, and in sin my mother conceived me.*
—PSALM 51:1–5

The third accusation is *iniquity*—the main one. *Sin* is about intent. *Transgression* is about activity. *Iniquity* is the sin in our bloodline. People try to explain away generational curses as they're not a popular teaching. They call it addiction or a generational habit. It's still a curse, I don't care what it's called. If it's working against someone and against the family, the bottom line is that it is still in operation. How does that work? Iniquity is in the bloodline; it's not just about a personal sin; it is about what's in the bloodline, passed on from one generation to the next.

Iniquity's consequences are fourfold:

1.  It gives the enemy a **legal right to tempt you** in a given area. Almost all strongholds come from an iniquitous route—almost all.

2.  Iniquity will **fashion your identity and the way you think about yourself,** if you let it. Isaiah says in Isaiah 6:5, *"Woe is me, for I am undone!"* Then he says when he hears God talking, his spiritual senses are awakened, and the moment his iniquity is dealt with, he can hear more clearly. When he hears the Lord ask *"Whom shall I send, and who will go for Us?"* Isaiah responds, *"Here am I! Send me"* (Isa. 6:6–8). All of a sudden Isaiah went from worrying about being destroyed to someone willing to be God's prophet. What happened? Iniquity was dealt with and his true identity emerged.

3. Iniquity undealt with **will detour you from your destiny**. Psalm 139:16 says that before you existed on earth, your days were described in a scroll, a book, in Heaven. On the day you were born, you weren't just a sweet little baby birthed on earth; you were also a scroll that landed in a family on earth. But here's the problem—you landed in a body connected to a bloodline. And the enemy uses the iniquity of your bloodline to try to pull you off course from what you were originally meant to accomplish. Many of the people living under bridges or on the streets today because of alcoholism, drug addiction, mental illness, or whatever were destined to cure illnesses, solve national or worldwide problems, or make other major breakthroughs. But the adversary used the iniquity in their bloodlines to pull them off course, preventing them from realizing their real purpose and destiny.

4. Iniquity is used by the enemy to **build cases against you in the courts of Heaven**. In 2 Samuel 21, there had been a famine in the land for three years. After the third year, King David asked the Lord why there was a famine. The Lord answered that his predecessor, Saul, 70 years prior, broke the covenant with the Gideonites that Joshua had made. Because of that broken covenant, the enemy had a legal right to bring famine to the land for three years. God told David that if he wanted God to answer his prayers for the land, he would have to go back into the history of Israel and deal with the broken covenant. So David asked the Gideonites about it and made it right; and the Bible says God heeded the prayer for the land. All the prayers that had been prayed for three years were null and void. But suddenly, when the legal issue was dealt with, the prayer was immediately answered.

You have to know how to undo the legal case against you if you want God to answer your prayers. If you have been praying prayers for a long time and there's been no answer, it's because something legal is standing in your way. The good news is that you have an Advocate in the court of Heaven who is actually pleading on your behalf, making intercession for you. God wants to answer your prayers. You are *not* dealing with an unwilling God; you are dealing with cases made against you from a ruthless accuser.

You have an advocate in Christ Jesus, and His blood speaks on your behalf! Even though this is a reality, it is also something you need to agree with and execute on your behalf in order for it to be effectual over your life and circumstances.

# REFLECTION

Pray and ask the Holy Spirit to reveal any evidences of iniquity operating in your life (based on the listed criteria). As you do this, protect your heart from condemnation.

Remember, Jesus is your advocate in the court of Heaven! God Almighty wants to answer your prayers, as that is His passion. The key is identifying any hindrances operating against you. The Holy Spirit wants you to recognize such things for one key purpose—displacing and dissolving them in the courts of Heaven!

# YOUR ADVOCATE IN THE COURTS OF HEAVEN: JESUS

*And the Lord said, "Simon, Simon! Indeed, Satan has asked for you, that he may sift you as wheat. But I have prayed for you, that your faith should not fail; and when you have returned to Me, strengthen your brethren."*
—LUKE 22:31-32

When I say to the Judge in the courts of Heaven, "I'm asking for this part of my destiny to become a reality," the adversary says, "He cannot have that. I have a case that says he is disqualified from having what You said about him before time began." This is why we feel frustrated; there's a case against us in Heaven just like there was against Peter, but Jesus says, *I have prayed for you.*

### JESUS STEPPED INTO THE COURTS OF HEAVEN ON OUR BEHALF.

In Jesus' earthly ministry, He did nothing as God and everything as man. He had not yet been qualified to be the High Priest because He had not yet fully completed God's purpose for Him being on the earth, which was dying on the cross and then being resurrected. So whenever Jesus stepped in and said *I have prayed for you,* He did not do that as God. He did that as a Man filled with God. When Jesus went to the court of Heaven on behalf of Peter and pled his case, that means we can too. In fact, we *have* to do it if we're going to see breakthrough in our lives, in our families, in our churches, in our cities, in our states, in our prophets, and in our nations.

For God to change the world, God's people must know how to go into the courts and deal in that realm so that what's written in the books of Heaven can be fleshed out on the earth. That's what we're here to do.

Courtroom activity is always connected to what's written in the books of destiny, which is why we need to know what's written in the books. We need prophetic understanding, prophetic revelation of what's in the books. This is another way of saying, *"Your kingdom come, Your will be done on earth as it is in Heaven"* (Matt. 6:10). We are pulling out of Heaven what's in Heaven and causing it to manifest on the earth. We're calling what's in the books into a fleshed-out demonstration on earth.

Next week, you will be introduced to what these books are and, specifically, what they contain. For now, it's important that you know this much: they contain revelation of your destiny that the devil wishes to oppose and thwart from coming to pass. The longer he can restrain the people of God from fulfilling the will of God written in the books of Heaven, the longer he *thinks* he can wreak havoc on earth. The fact is, God's will *is going to be done*. The opportunity we have is to participate in His will by executing it through fulfilling what's written in our books.

## BIBLE STUDY

Read Luke 22:31-32.

Explain how Jesus acts as your advocate in the court of Heaven, praying for you when the adversary is trying to bring a case against you.

_____

_____

_____

_____

_____

_____

_____

_____

_____

_____

_____

_____

# SESSION NOTES

# Session 3

# YOUR BOOK OF DESTINY IN HEAVEN

*The court was seated, and the books were opened.*
—DANIEL 7:10

When the Bible says *the books are opened,* you need to understand there are all sorts of books in Heaven—the Book of Life for example. Whatever happens in the court will happen from the books, because the Bible says the court is seated and the books are opened. Why are the books open? Because many of the books are books of destiny.

## SUMMARY

You will have clear vision of how to break off curses and iniquity in the bloodline when you understand that the enemy is warring against what's written in your book in Heaven. He knows that when you fulfill what's recorded in your book, the purposes of God will come to pass in the earth.

The following session will serve as an introductory study of Scripture describing the books of destiny written and recorded in Heaven. You will receive a Bible blueprint for what these books of destiny are and how what's written in these books is directly connected to the activity that takes place in the courts of Heaven.

Finally, you will receive an evaluation tool that will help you identify whether or not you are presently walking in your calling and destiny.

# INTERACTIVE QUESTIONS

> **IT TAKES COURTROOM OPERATION AND ACTIVITY TO GET THE DESTINY THAT GOD HAS FOR US.**

1. Read Daniel 7:10.

   *A fiery stream issued and came forth from before Him. A thousand thousands ministered to Him; ten thousand times ten thousand stood before Him. The court was seated, and the books were opened* (Daniel 7:10).

   Describe the language in this passage that points to "books in Heaven."

   _____

   _____

   _____

   _____

   _____

   _____

2. How does the court of Heaven render verdicts *with* human participation?

   _____

   _____

   _____

   _____

   _____

   _____

> ## THE COURT OF HEAVEN CANNOT RENDER VERDICTS WITHOUT HUMAN ACTIVITY AND PARTICIPATION.

3.  Read Daniel 7:25–27.

> *He shall speak pompous words against the Most High, shall persecute the saints of the Most High, and shall intend to change times and law. Then the saints shall be given into his hand for a time and times and half a time. But the court shall be seated, and they shall take away his dominion, to consume and destroy it forever. Then the kingdom and dominion, and the greatness of the kingdoms under the whole heaven, shall be given to the people, the saints of the Most High. His kingdom is an everlasting kingdom, and all dominions shall serve and obey Him* (Daniel 7:25–27).

How can verdicts from the court of Heaven bring you out of defeat and into victory?

4.  Read Daniel 7:9-10.

> *I watched till thrones were put in place, and the Ancient of Days was seated; His garment was white as snow, and the hair of His head was like pure wool. His throne was a fiery flame, its wheels a burning fire; a fiery stream issued and came forth from before Him. A thousand thousands ministered to Him; ten thousand times ten thousand stood before Him.* **The court was seated, and the books were opened** (Daniel 7:9-10).

Describe the important connection between what happens in the court of Heaven and what is written in the books.

_____

_____

_____

_____

_____

_____

_____

_____

_____

_____

_____

> **THERE WAS A BOOK IN HEAVEN WRITTEN ABOUT YOU BEFORE TIME BEGAN.**

5. Read Psalm 139:16.

   *Your eyes saw my substance, being yet unformed. And in Your book they all were written, the days fashioned for me, when as yet there were none of them* (Psalm 139:16).

   How does this verse of Scripture describe the *books of destiny* in Heaven?

_____

_____

_____

_____

_____

_____

6. How do you understand the following statement: Destiny is not something you create; destiny is something that you discover.

7. Read 2 Timothy 1:9.

    *Who has saved us and called us with a holy calling, not according to our works, but according to His own purpose and grace which was given to us in Christ Jesus before time began* (2 Timothy 1:9).

    What does it mean for your purpose to have "grace attached to it"? How does this *grace* indicate that you are walking in your calling and destiny?

8. How does the devil try to prevent God's purposes from coming to pass in the earth? How does this specifically relate to you and your unique book of destiny?

_____

_____

_____

_____

_____

_____

_____

_____

_____

_____

9. By what standard will we be judged for our lives on earth?

_____

_____

_____

_____

_____

_____

_____

_____

_____

# ACTIVATION EXERCISE:
# INDICATORS THAT YOU'VE DISCOVERED YOUR
# PURPOSE AND ARE WALKING IN YOUR DESTINY

**Take this time to personally evaluate if you are walking in your calling and destiny.** When this is evaluation is conducted, usually a strong percentage of those in attendance raise their hands, indicating that they do not live with a clear sense of calling, purpose, or destiny. And these audiences consist of Spirit-filled believers!

**Don't let the devil make you feel condemned about this!** The truth is, the overwhelming majority of people on the earth live disconnected from their destinies—believers and unbelievers alike. When we live disconnected from destiny, unfortunately, it is easy for us to become landing places for the strategies of the adversary, which include iniquity, sin, and transgression. Curses in our lives and bloodlines continue to perpetuate this disconnection.

In addition, when we live disconnected from a clear sense of calling or purpose, we begin to live visionless lives, and where there is no vision people perish because they cast off restraint (see Prov. 29:18). When we live without a vision of what's written in our book of destiny, there will be no sense of order or structure to how we conduct ourselves.

On the contrary, when you have a glimpse of destiny you will live motivated to resist temptation and steward every moment of your life, driven by a clear sense of purpose.

## *Evaluation*

The following are indicators that you've discovered your purpose. If you cannot answer these completely or have a difficult time with this exercise, this might be an indicator that you need to have your book of destiny opened. In future sessions, you will receive specific instruction on how to engage this process.

1. **You enjoy it...**because grace is attached to it.

   You can even *enjoy* a job or season in life that is not comfortable or favorable because, even though you're not in your ideal position vocationally, you live aware that God has you on the path of destiny.

   Do you enjoy what you're doing now?

Do you live with an overall sense of joy and fulfillment, or do you feel like everything is a fight?

Do you find peace in where you are right now, or do you live under the impression that the "next place" or "promotion" or "next season" will be what brings you fulfillment?

Do you experience an overall sense of purpose and destiny where you are, right now, or are you simply tolerating it?

2. **You will be good at it…**you will be graced with giftings and talents for what you're doing.

   Do you feel a particular gifting or talent for what you are doing right now?

   Regardless of your present place of employment or vocation, are there specific gifts and talents God has entrusted to you that you can use in your current position—right now?

   Take a brief inventory of some of the things you are involved with in life—activities, job, volunteering, etc. Which of these activities have unique grace on them?

   Finally, be very honest with yourself. Are there things you're presently involved with that you do **not** have a talent for, and yet you're doing them out of a sense of obligation? Perhaps you're doing them to be recognized or noticed? Perhaps you're doing them because you **think** you're good at them when, in fact, there are actually gifts and talents stored up within you that have grace on them.

_____

Be honest in this process. Resist the enemy's condemnation, but do not be afraid of honest, self-evaluation. Where do you see God's grace upon your talent and giftings? This is, most likely, a clue to your destiny and calling!

3. **You will have success doing it…**because the grace attached to what you're doing will produce fruitfulness.

   Ask the Holy Spirit to show you the gifts and talents He has placed within you.

   Make a list of these, and then write some of the "success stories" that functioning in these talents has produced. You don't necessarily have to be overly spiritual when describing the "fruitfulness" that operating in your giftings has produced. Simply pay attention to the impact that these giftings have had on other people, the community, business, etc.

_____

4. **You will be able to make money doing it…**because God wants you to make money doing what you're passionate about.

Would you honestly say that you are currently making money for what you are passionate about?

If you do not feel like what you are currently doing as a job intersects with your "passions," gifts, and talents, pause for a moment. Ask the Holy Spirit to show you how you can use your giftings in the place where you currently are.

Write down what He shares with you, as it is very important for the body of Christ to live motivated by a sense of destiny and assignment, even when they are doing jobs that do not appear to be "perfect."

Write down some of the dreams and goals you have and how these intersect with your gifts/talents. How would these dreams/goals coming to pass actually make you money?

5. **The right people will bear witness to you…** because the grace of God is visible on your life.

    Write down any confirmations or encouragements you have received from people indicating that you're walking in your assignment/destiny.

    Pause and carefully consider this.

    Prayerfully reflect upon words of encouragement, words of prophecy, and any other indicators you have received from people—both those close to you and maybe those who barely know you—that you are walking in divine destiny or that your destiny might be linked to something specific that needs to be unlocked. (Prophetic words will typically direct you toward something that might need to be unlocked for you to begin walking in your destiny).

Again, if you struggled answering these questions, it might indicate that you need to come before the court of Heaven and ask for your destiny to be unlocked and revealed. This is actually a good sign, because God wants to make this information known to you! You will be able to walk through this transformational process in an upcoming session.

This is not a process that will leave you with more answers than questions; if anything, it is purposed to confront the delay that seems to be restraining you from walking in a sense of fulfillment and purpose.

We will repeat this exercise at the conclusion of the interactive manual, as this is a very effective inventory tool for you to use on a reoccurring basis.

# THE BOOKS IN HEAVEN

*Your [God's] eyes saw my substance, being yet unformed. And in Your book they all were written, the days fashioned for me, when as yet there were none of them.*
—PSALM 139:16

David is writing about the books of destiny in this often cited passage of Scripture. He basically says that before he existed on the earth, there was a book in Heaven about him. The same is true for you!

You didn't just appear on earth without thought or reason. There is, and always was, a book in Heaven written about you before time began. What is in that book? David said very clearly that God saw his substance—God saw *him* through and through. What does that mean? God not only knew what David would look like, He knew his DNA—why David would like certain things and not like other things. Why he would be attracted to this and not that. God made David unique. Likewise, He made you unique. Your God-crafted and designed DNA makes you who you are. You are unique!

What is written in the book of Heaven about you is important because God knew you before you were even born and He fashioned your days. What does that mean? God already knew the span of time you will live on the earth and what you are supposed to accomplish for the Kingdom during that time. That's what's in the book of Heaven that is opened in the courts of Heaven.

Some people think God's going to make you do something you don't like. No, He won't. He made you in a certain way to be attracted to certain things and if, for whatever reason, iniquity has warped that, Jesus will come in and save you and change you so that you like what He likes and want what He wants. That's the way it works. Everything written in the book of Heaven is about your destiny, your purpose.

Remember:

**DESTINY IS NOT SOMETHING YOU CREATE—
DESTINY IS SOMETHING YOU DISCOVER..**

# REFLECTION QUESTION

Explain your understanding of what the *books in Heaven* are.

_____

_____

_____

_____

_____

_____

_____

_____

_____

How are these books related to your personal destiny?

_____

_____

_____

_____

_____

_____

_____

_____

_____

_____

# HIS PURPOSE, HIS GRACE

*God, who has saved us and called us with a holy calling, not
according to our works, but according to His own purpose and grace
which was given to us in Christ Jesus before time began.*
—2 TIMOTHY 1:8-9

In 2 Timothy 1:9, Paul says that we are not called *"according to our works,"* or in other words we didn't impress God and God decided He liked us. He said we are not called according to *our works* but according to *"His own purpose and grace which was given to us in Christ Jesus before time began."* Purpose and grace was given to us in Christ Jesus? When? Before time began! Before there was a moon, before there were stars and a sun, before there was anything that creates time—before any of that existed, God gave us purpose and grace.

> **OUR PURPOSE AND HIS GRACE HAVE BEEN WAITING
> TO BE DISCOVERED SINCE BEFORE TIME BEGAN.**

What does that mean? You will know when you have discovered your purpose because it will feel right—you will have the skills and talents to fulfill it. After all, it has been written in the book and is your destiny; it's why you're here. You will also know you have discovered your purpose because of the grace attached. Purpose and grace go together; so if there is no grace attached to what you think is your purpose, it's not your purpose.

I'm trying to help you discover why you were born. God purposed you before time began and even wrote about you in the book. When you start piecing this all together, it clearly says that before time began, in the book of Heaven your destiny, your purpose was already settled in God's mind and will.

So why are you here?

---

**YOU ARE HERE TO FLESH OUT ON THE EARTH WHAT'S BEEN WRITTEN ABOUT YOU IN THE BOOK OF HEAVEN.**

---

But guess what? The devil doesn't want that to happen because if enough of us get fleshed out on the earth what's written in the books of Heaven about us, God's purpose is going to be accomplished. *The enemy's best way to stop God's purpose from being done is to stop us from discovering and carrying out our destiny.*

## BIBLE STUDY

Read 2 Timothy 1:8-9.

Describe your understanding of God's purpose and grace when it comes to your calling/destiny.

_____

_____

_____

_____

_____

_____

_____

_____

_____

_____

_____

_____

_____

_____

_____

_____

_____

_____

# HOW DO YOU DISCOVER YOUR DESTINY?

*God who works in you to will and to act in order to fulfill his good purpose.*
—PHILIPPIANS 2:13 NIV

Whatever your purpose is, you'll know it's your purpose because of the grace attached. You may wonder, *How do I know if there's grace attached to what I think my destiny is?* To answer that question, there are five signs that indicate grace is attached to your purpose:

1. **Your purpose *will be enjoyable* if it has grace attached**. There may be things about it you don't enjoy, but overall you enjoy what your purpose is because it has grace attached to it. Jesus is not sentencing you to a life of misery. You won't be thinking, *Well I guess I'm just going to have to go to that foreign nation and be a missionary.* No! You're not going to have to do anything that you don't feel excited about. You'll either like it or you'll change your heart to like it because it is ***"God who works in you** to will and to act in order **to fulfill his good purpose"*** (Phil. 2:13 NIV).

2. The second sign that you've discovered your purpose with grace attached is that not only will you enjoy it but **you'll be good at it.** Why will you be good at it? Because grace is always connected to gifts. You will grow in your ability to fulfill your purpose. You get better at it. Whatever you're graced to do, whatever your purpose is that has grace attached, you will find you have gifts that make you good at what God has called you to do and created you for. And the more you do it, the better you become—you will be good at it.

3. Whatever you've been graced to do that's connected to your purpose, **you will have *success* doing it**. This is different from being good at it. You will have success. Now be careful with this one, because sometimes God doesn't define success the way we do. Maybe I should say you will be *fruitful* in your purpose. There will be fruit; whatever your purpose is that has grace attached, as you are faithful in the little, He will add

and bring increase. There will be success and fruitfulness attached to whatever your graced purpose is.

4. Whatever your purpose is that has grace attached, **you will make money**. God knows you need money to provide for you and your family. I've never met anyone who was so spiritual that they didn't need money to live day to day. Here's the truth: it is enjoyable to make money with what you're passionate about. I know many people who have spent their whole lives just going to work, just getting by making a living—but they had no passion for it. That's a miserable life. God wants you to make a living doing what you're passionate about, and if you set your heart toward Him, He will make that a reality.

5. Whatever your purpose is that has grace attached, **the right people will bear witness to you.** I didn't say everybody will. Some won't like you regardless of what you do or don't do. You'll always have the naysayers; you'll even have enemies; but God will make sure the right people bear witness to you. For instance, Jesus had John the Baptist who bore witness to Him. John the Baptist could see who Jesus was before anybody else could. There will always be those who will recognize the grace on your life. Paul and Barnabas had Peter and John, Cephas and John, who saw the grace of God that was upon them. They extended the right hand of fellowship and consequently they could launch into their apostolic ministry on a platform not available to them prior. Not everybody bore witness to them, but the right ones could see who they were. God will see to it that the right ones can see who you are. Not everybody, but the right ones.

Over the next two days, you will prayerfully work through these five signs.

# THREE PRACTICAL KEYS TO DISCOVERING YOUR DESTINY AND CALLING

These five signs can help you discern what's in your book in Heaven! Today, you will review the first three in this interactive exercise.

Use each of the three categories to evaluate your own life's calling and purpose. Use the following pages to interact with these three criteria and ask the Holy Spirit to help you discern what areas in your life (gifts, talents, abilities) have supernatural grace attached.

## YOUR PURPOSE WILL BE ENJOYABLE

Is what you are presently doing/pursuing enjoyable? When using your gifts and talents, do you get a sense of enjoyment and fulfillment out of it?

## YOU WILL BE GOOD AT WHAT YOU ARE DOING

Are you effective and excellent in doing what you perceive you are gifted/talented to do? Ask the Holy Spirit to help realistically lead you to identify what you are good at/what you are not good at. We need to be honest in our evaluation, as we are will not be good at *everything*.

# YOU WILL HAVE SUCCESS DOING IT

Are you successful in doing what you are gifted/talented to do? Even though monetary success is one dimension of this, are lives being impacted and enriched? Do you see measurable good fruit? Are you satisfied and fulfilled as a result of doing what you're doing?

# TWO PRACTICAL KEYS TO DISCOVERING YOUR DESTINY AND CALLING

These five signs can help you discern what's in your book in Heaven! Today, you will review the final two by going through this interactive exercise.

Use each of the two categories to evaluate your own life's calling and purpose. Use the following pages to interact with these two criteria and ask the Holy Spirit to help you discern what areas in your life (gifts, talents, abilities) have supernatural grace attached.

### *You Will Make Money Doing It*

God desires for you to experience convergence in your life where what you enjoy doing is actually what creates financial wealth and provision for you. Do you currently see this intersection in your life, where your gifts/talents bring about financial increase? Discuss.

### The Right People Will Bear Witness to You

In this final category, ask the Holy Spirit to bring to remembrance any words of encouragement, exhortations, and prophetic words that have been released over you concerning certain gifts, talents, and abilities. This may take some time and research, but is definitely worth it. The goal is to prayerfully identify what these trusted individuals were calling *out of you* through their encouragements and prophetic words. And of course, make sure that those who released these words over you are trustworthy individuals who have the right to speak into your life, even correctively.

# Session 4

# WHAT'S WRITTEN IN YOUR BOOK OF DESTINY?

## SUMMARY

The purposes of God being fulfilled are directly linked to His people fulfilling individual destinies. As what's written about in the books of Heaven comes to pass through the people of God, the purposes of God are advanced, the Kingdom of God is established, and the reign of God is released.

God's will shall be accomplished in the world, one way or the other. However, He has established an authority structure in the earth realm that involves human participation with divine purposes.

In this session, you will discover how to discern what's recorded in your book of destiny, specifically using Jesus as the key example. Even though Jesus was, is, and forever will be the eternal Son of God, He also took on the identity of *Son of Man*. He did this to perfectly identify with human beings, providing all believers a repeatable example to follow in their everyday lives.

## INTERACTIVE QUESTIONS

1. Describe your understanding of how the devil can postpone the plans of God from being accomplished on earth?

_____

_____

_____

_____

> **THE PURPOSE OF GOD IN THE EARTH IS CONNECTED TO HIS PEOPLE FULFILLING THEIR DESTINY.**

2. What happens when the books of destiny are opened? What impact does this have on the spirit realm?

_____

_____

_____

_____

_____

_____

_____

3. Explain how there is a case against you if you have a Kingdom purpose.

_____

_____

_____

_____

_____

4. Read Psalm 40:6–8.

*Sacrifice and offering You did not desire; my ears You have opened. Burnt offering and sin offering You did not require. Then I said, "Behold, I come; in the scroll of the book it is written of me. I delight to do Your will, O my God, and Your law is within my heart"* (Psalm 40:6–8).

How do these passages in the Book of Psalms point to Jesus's book of destiny in Heaven?

5. Describe how you can use Psalm 40:6–8 as a blueprint for discerning what's in your book of destiny (because Jesus is your example).

6. Why is it important to develop a "prophetic ear" in order to access what's written in your book of destiny?

7. Describe the relationship between prophecy and books of destiny.

8.  Explain how what's written in your book of destiny is also written on your heart.

9.  How does the ability to dream access what's written in your book of destiny?

# ACTIVATION EXERCISE:
## TUNING IN TO THE PROPHETIC AND RESTORING YOUR ABILITY TO DREAM

To access what is written in your book of destiny, there are two key areas that will help give you understanding—the prophetic and the ability to dream. Both of these are under significant attack, as they are instrumental in connecting people on earth to destinies that are recorded in the heavenly realms.

Both dreaming and the prophetic are bridges that connect people with a revelation of destiny.

In this activation exercise, I want you—using the very Scriptures that Jesus cited—to open your ears to hear the prophetic word of the Lord and also seek out what has been written in your heart.

**1. *Tuning In to the Prophetic***

*Sacrifice and offering You did not desire; my ears You have opened* (Psalm 40:6).

Prayer:

*Father, right now I ask You to open my ears to hear Your prophetic word. Right now, I come against any hindrance that is preventing me from hearing Your freshly spoken word. I recognize that it is Your will for all believers to prophesy and hear prophetically. This includes me!*

*Lord, I repent for giving my ear-gates and eye-gates to anything unclean.*

*I repent for dismissing Your voice speaking to me through signs, symbols, pictures, or unusual occurrences.*

*I repent for making declarations or confessions, actually saying things like, "I am not a prophet" or "I don't hear God that way" or "I don't have visions and dreams." On the basis of your Word, the very signs of Holy Spirit outpouring are the prophetic, dreams, and visions. These were not limited to a specific group of Christians—they are available to all who have received the Holy Spirit. I have the Holy Spirit, so I have access to the prophetic voice of God!*

*Open my eyes and ears that I might see and hear You, Lord!*

**2. *Restoring Your Ability to Dream***

*I delight to do Your will, O my God, and Your law is within my heart* (Psalm 40:8).

*God, I recognize that Your law is written on the tablet of my heart. In fact, Your Word says that eternity is written on my heart.*

*Everything that You have purposed for me to do, to accomplish, and to fulfill has been written on the scroll of my heart.*

*I repent for embracing anything in my life that has hindered or even extinguished the ability to dream.*

*I repent for placing boundaries and barriers around my dreams, only conceiving of things that I can accomplish in my own ability or strength. Connect me, Holy Spirit, with the dreams that only Christ in me can bring to pass!*

*Even now, Holy Spirit, I ask You to release a fresh flow of dreams in the night and visions in the day. Help me to take the limitations off my imagination.*

*If I have been afraid of venturing into the realm of imagination, right now I place my imagination and dream life under the sanctifying influence of the Holy Spirit. Release me from any fear of dreaming, and I ask You to connect me with the very purposes You've written on my heart through the conduit of dreaming.*

# SESSION NOTES

# JESUS, YOUR MODEL

*Let this mind be in you which was also in Christ Jesus, who, being in the form of God, did not consider it robbery to be equal with God, but made Himself of no reputation, taking the form of a bondservant, and coming in the likeness of men. And being found in appearance as a man, He humbled Himself and became obedient to the point of death, even the death of the cross.*
—Philippians 2:5–8

Jesus had to be just like us. A human lost creation, so a human had to win it back. So when Jesus came to earth, He did nothing as God. That statement may surprise you, but He never did anything as God. He did do everything as a Man filled with God. He was, is, and forever will be God.

You see, if He did anything as God, He disqualified Himself from being our Savior. That's why Jesus could say, *"and they will do even greater things than these, because I am going to the Father"* (John 14:12 NIV). Jesus was saying, in essence, "Look, everything I've done I've done as a Man filled with God. I am releasing the same Holy Spirit to you, so you are going to be people filled with God; so the same works I have done, you're going to do and do even greater things than what I did."

Philippians 2:5–11 says that Jesus humbled Himself, coming in the likeness of men, in absolute surrender to the Father so that He fulfilled the total will and purpose of God in His life while on earth. He did everything as a Man filled with God, not as God. His purpose for doing that *was to fulfill what was written in a volume of the book that's in Heaven before time began.*

Jesus' purpose for coming to earth was to fulfill what was in the book. Why? Because that's our purpose on the earth—to fulfill what's been written in the book of Heaven about us. That's why we're here. That is why John 1:14 says, among other things, *Jesus is the Word made flesh.* What does that mean? Well it could mean that He came to earth to flesh out on the earth the word written about Him in Heaven.

> **WE ARE LIVING ON THE EARTH TO FLESH OUT ON EARTH THE WORD WRITTEN ABOUT US IN HEAVEN BEFORE TIME BEGAN.**

That's why I am here. That's why you're here!

# BIBLE STUDY

Review Philippians 2:5–8.

Why do you think it was so important for Jesus to function as a *man* while living on earth instead of functioning as God? (Remember, Jesus was always God—He never stopped being God, but He did lay aside His divine privileges as God and instead operated on earth as a man *filled* with God.)

# WHAT'S WRITTEN IN YOUR BOOK?

*Then I said, "Behold, I have come—in the volume of the book*
*it is written of Me—to do Your will, O God."*
—HEBREWS 10:7

Anything that has a Kingdom purpose has a book in Heaven about it. Whether an individual, a family line, a church, a culture, a business, a city, a province, a state, a nation, etc.

If there's a Kingdom purpose for it, there's a book in Heaven about it. If there is no book in Heaven about it, don't waste your time on it because it has no Kingdom value. It has no Kingdom purpose. Every person who ever lived has a book in Heaven about them.

**IT'S UP TO EACH INDIVIDUAL TO DISCERN
WHAT'S IN HIS OR HER BOOK AND FULFILL IT.**

I believe when we stand before the Lord we will give an account of how much of our books we have fulfilled or not fulfilled. That's what our judgment will really be based on—not this little sin and that little sin—rather, how much of what was written in our books did we accomplish. How much did we get done that God committed us to before the foundations of the earth? We need to discover what's in our books and begin to flesh it out.

Now, how can that be? The Bible says that *even Jesus has a book in Heaven about Him.* Hebrews 10:5–7 says:

*Therefore, when He [Jesus] came into the world, He said [about Himself]: "Sacrifice and offering You did not desire, but a body You have prepared for Me. In burnt offerings and sacrifices for sin You had no pleasure. Then I said, 'Behold, I have come—in the volume of* ***the book it is written of Me****—to do Your will, O God.'"*

In other words, God no longer wants the offerings connected to the Old Covenant—no bulls and goats and other animals. God made Jesus a human body to offer as a living sacrifice on the cross. Jesus is saying that His purpose for coming in a human body was to fulfill what was written in a book in Heaven about Him. Jesus said His reason for existence on the earth was to fulfill the will of God written in a book in Heaven about Him. That was His reason for coming.

# BIBLE STUDY

Read Hebrews 10:5–7.

Explain your understanding of this concept: you will be judged (evaluated) based on what you fulfill in your book of destiny.

_____

_____

_____

_____

_____

_____

_____

_____

_____

_____

_____

_____

_____

_____

_____

_____

_____

_____

_____

# HOW TO DISCERN WHAT IS IN YOUR BOOK OF DESTINY

*Sacrifice and offering You did not desire; my ears You have opened. Burnt offering and sin offering You did not require. Then I said, "Behold, I come; in the scroll of the book it is written of me. I delight to do Your will, O my God, and Your law is within my heart"*
*—PSALM 40:6–8*

How do we understand what's written in the books of Heaven about us? First of all, we need to understand that Jesus knew what was written in the books of Heaven about Him. Remember that Jesus is Son of God and Son of Man. He was and is eternally God, but He also walked the earth as a Spirit-filled man, modeling to mankind what life would look like. He is both mankind's Messiah and Model. With this in mind, consider how Jesus had an awareness of what was in His book of destiny.

Psalm 40:6–8 is the original place from which Hebrews 10:5–7 was written. The writer of Hebrews was quoting Psalm 40 when he wrote, *"Behold, I have come—in the volume of the book to do Your will, O God."* But the psalmist says in Psalm 40:6–8:

> *Sacrifice and offering You did not desire; my ears You have opened. Burnt offering and sin offering You did not require. Then I said, "Behold, I come; in the scroll of the book it is written of me. I delight to do Your will, O my God, and Your law is within my heart."*

## HOW TO DISCERN WHAT'S IN YOUR BOOK:

First of all Jesus says, "My ears You have opened."

1.  To know what's in your book, you have to develop a prophetic ear.

He was saying, "My ears You have opened. You have awakened prophetic abilities in me." You will never discern what's in your book in the natural. You have to discern it out of the spirit. So, you need to pray, "Lord, awaken my prophetic ability." I believe that we are moving into a new time of greater prophetic abilities.

Zechariah, a bone fide prophet, says in the Bible that *"The angel who talked with me came back and wakened me, as a man who is wakened out of his sleep"* (Zech. 4:1). And he saw these visions now because he was awakened to a new dimension. What does that mean? That means that the angel of awakening showed up and awakened Zachariah's prophetic abilities to a new dimension. I believe with every part of my being that angels have been released, even an angel of awakening, that are waking up the body of Christ to brand-new dimensions of the prophetic.

Second, Psalm 40:7-8 says, *"in the scroll of the book it is written of me. I delight to do Your will, O my God, and Your law is within my heart."*

2. Whatever God wrote in the book of Heaven about you, know too that *He also wrote it in your heart.*

You do not need to go to Heaven to read it, even though if you can and you want to, great. But you don't have to because whatever God wrote in your book, He also wrote it as a law in your heart.

# Session 5

# RETRIEVING AND UNLOCKING YOUR BOOK

Until you have possession of your book of destiny and your book is opened so you can know what's in it, you cannot present cases in the courts of Heaven. Cases in the courts of Heaven have to be presented from revelation of what's recorded in your book. That's why Daniel 7:10 says *the court was seated and the books were opened*. What's going to take place in the courts of Heaven takes place based on what's in the books.

So here's the problem. Some people, even though there's a book about them in Heaven, do not have possession of their book. Some nations do not have possession of their books, some churches, and on and on. How can that be? Because someone in the family bloodline or something in the history of the country caused the book to be sold.

For example, Esau had a book in Heaven about him. He was the firstborn. He had an inheritance from God based on who he was. But guess what happened—he sold his book. When he was hungry he sold his book for a bowl of porridge. Then guess what happened—when he sold his book, he also sold his family's book, his family line, because he was a father of a nation. A whole family can lose its destiny because its book has been sold as a result of someone in the history of that family making an agreement with a satanic power that allowed it to take possession of that family's book.

## SUMMARY

This is one of the most important sessions, as you will learn the process of how to retrieve and open your book of destiny. Up until this point, you have been receiving foundational instruction in the courts

97

of Heaven prayer strategy and an introduction of books of destiny. Now, you will learn how to put these revelatory strategies into practice.

You will be introduced to two distinct processes for two groups of people. First, there are those who feel like they have no sense of destiny. For this group, they actually need to retrieve their book of destiny. Most often, the reason these individuals feel like they have no sense of destiny, purpose, or calling is because their books of destiny have been "sold out" through bloodline curses. Once the bloodline issues are dealt with, books can be retrieved.

Second, there are those who live with a vague sense of destiny, but there is no clarity on what it is or how it should be expressed. In illustrated form, it's like they have access to their books of destiny, but the books remain closed. The material in this session will also help participants learn how to open and unlock what's written in their books if they fall into this specific category.

## INTERACTIVE QUESTIONS

1. How are you supposed to present cases in the court of Heaven? What serves as the foundation for your case?

_____

_____

_____

_____

> **PEOPLE DON'T HAVE ACCESS TO THEIR BOOK BECAUSE SOMETHING IN THE _BLOODLINE_ SOLD THE BOOK OUT.**

2. Describe how "bloodline curses" can sell out our books of destiny.

_____

_____

_____

_____

_____

3. Explain the two indicators that reveal your family's book of destiny has been sold out.

   a. You have no sense of destiny:

   b. Sin in the family line:

4. What is the difference between retrieving your book and unlocking/opening your book?

5. Read Isaiah 29:10.

   *For the Lord has poured out on you the spirit of deep sleep, and has closed your eyes, namely, the prophets; and He has covered your heads, namely, the seers* (Isaiah 29:10).

   Describe how prophetic revelation opens the books of Heaven.

6. Read Isaiah 29:11-12.

*The whole vision has become to you like the words of a book that is sealed, which men deliver to one who is literate, saying, "Read this, please." And he says, "I cannot, for it is sealed." Then the book is delivered to one who is illiterate, saying, "Read this, please." And he says, "I am not literate"* (Isaiah 29:11-12).

Why is it important for books of destiny to be *open* in order for people and prophets to receive prophetic insight?

_____

_____

_____

_____

_____

Articulate your understanding of the five principles to opening and unlocking your book of destiny.

_____

_____

_____

_____

_____

7. Read Isaiah 29:13.

*Therefore the Lord said: "Inasmuch as these people draw near with their mouths and honor Me with their lips, but have removed their hearts far from Me, and their fear toward Me is taught by the commandment of men* (Isaiah 29:13).

How is *true worship* important to opening the books of heaven? Describe what this might look like.

_____

_____

_____

_____

8. Read Revelation 22:10.

   *And he said to me, "Do not seal the words of the prophecy of this book, for the time is at hand"* (Revelation 22:10).

   How do open books of destiny and increased prophetic revelation confirm that a shift has taken place in *timing*?

---

**HEAVEN CANNOT MOVE UNTIL BOOKS ARE OPEN.**

---

9. Explain how tears of *intercession* can open the books of Heaven.

**THE GOVERNMENTAL ROAR OF THE LION ALWAYS COMES OUT OF THE BROKENNESS OF THE LAMB.**

10. How is the *correct way* to approach the courts of Heaven? On what basis do you approach the courts? Explain why this is so important and how it will shift the way you pray.

_____

_____

_____

_____

_____

_____

_____

_____

_____

_____

_____

_____

# ACTIVATION EXERCISE 1: RETRIEVING YOUR BOOK OF DESTINY

1.  **Evaluate:** The first thing you must do is evaluate which category you fall under. It is possible that your book (or your family's book) of destiny has been sold out because something in the *bloodline* sold it out.

2.  **Ask yourself these essential questions...** and remember, you are the only one who will be reviewing this material. You must be as honest and transparent as possible.

    a.  *Do I have a sense of destiny?* If you do *not* feel like you have any sense of destiny, purpose, or meaning, it is very possible that, due to some kind of iniquity inherited through the bloodline, your book of destiny has been sold out and needs to be retrieved. This leads to the next question.

    b.  *Does my family line have a history of multiple expressions of sin—immorality, addiction, debauchery, etc.?* Prayerfully evaluate your family's history and consider any kind of recurring cases of sin and immorality that seem to be transferred from one generation to the next. This might require further investigation, but simply begin with asking the Holy Spirit to reveal any of these items to you. He does *not* want you to remain disconnected from your destiny because of any kind of generational, bloodline iniquity. Trust that He will reveal areas that need to be addressed and repented for.

3.  **Repent, renounce, and break agreement!** As the Holy Spirit reveals areas of bloodline iniquity that need to be confronted, feel free to list those below and, by name, break agreement with them through repentance and renunciation.

*Father, I come before You right now to confront the bloodline iniquities and sins that have been passed down generationally. Right now, I declare I am covered by the blood of Jesus. I declare that the blood of Jesus has made complete atonement, not only for my sins, but for the sin and bloodline iniquity I am going to list right now.*

*I repent and renounce... (list the specific areas that the Holy Spirit makes known to you).*

It's important to keep this written record, not to remind yourself of past sins or generational iniquities, but to remind the devil that repentance has been made for these items.

# ACTIVATION EXERCISE 2:
# UNLOCKING AND OPENING YOUR BOOK OF DESTINY

Perhaps you are not dealing with some of the hindering bloodline issues. Maybe you even feel like your book of destiny has been made available to you but it remains closed and inaccessible. In other words, you have a sense of destiny and purpose, but it's elusive—almost like you cannot put your finger on what you have been called to do.

This is where you would come into the courts of Heaven and unlock your book of destiny. In the video curriculum sessions, Robert Henderson leads you in prayers that take you through the process of entering the courts of Heaven to access what is written in your book of destiny.

Throughout the coming week, put into practice the five principles that will help to open and unlock your book. Cultivate them in your life and ask the Holy Spirit to give you additional insight on how these items can help open books of destiny.

1.  **True worship:** Cultivate a lifestyle of true, God-focused, Jesus-exalting worship.

2.  **Timing:** Recognize and respond to the timing and seasons of God.

3.  **Intercession:** Your prayers and intercessions have the ability to open books of Heaven over your life and also over other people, regions, and nations.

4.  **Approaching the courts of Heaven on the right basis:** Remember, you approach the courts of Heaven on the basis of God's purposes, not on the basis of your needs.

5.  **Apostolic decrees and authority:** When apostolic voices make decrees and release Kingdom authority, this has the ability to shift things in the spirit realm, thus opening the books in heaven.

# SESSION NOTES

# RETRIEVING YOUR BOOK OF DESTINY

*So I will restore to you the years that the swarming locust has eaten, the crawling locust, the consuming locust, and the chewing locust.*
—JOEL 2:25

There are two ways to you know if your family's book was sold, resulting in lifelong struggles for all family members.

Number 1: **You have no sense of destiny**. As hard as you may try to set a course for your life, deep down you have no real sense of destiny. You're told you're supposed to have destiny, but you end up doing good things—doing this and that, but honestly you don't feel that it's *the* thing you should be doing. It's just not you. You try to have one, but you just don't. It's amazing how many people in the body of Christ have no sense of destiny; and that's really frustrating because we're told we're supposed to have a sense of destiny, but we don't. We don't because somewhere in our family line our books were sold.

Number 2: The second sign that your book has been sold out is that **your whole family line has no sense of destiny**. Many have given themselves over to all sorts of debaucheries. Whether it's substance issue, substance control issues, sexual immorality, or whatever, your family has what the Bible calls "*the desolations of many generations*" (Isa. 61:4). Why would that be? Because *without a vision the people perish* (see Prov. 29:18). Remember that word? *Without a vision, they case off restraint*. Your family line is beset with all sorts of addictions and issues and immorality because your family line has no purpose or clear vision of destiny; in a time past, your book was sold to a demonic power, and you need to get it back.

I have good news for you! You can get it back. You can get your book back today, literally, because God wants you to have your book. He wants you to have the sense of destiny that goes with having your book. Retrieving your book is the first challenge we're going to deal with.

# REFLECTION

Ask the Holy Spirit to reveal to you any areas where your book of destiny/family's book of destiny might have been sold out.

Use the two indicators presented today to help you evaluate:

1.  Do you feel like you have a clear sense of destiny? Explain.

_____

_____

_____

_____

_____

_____

2.  Observe your family line. Do you notice common, recurring patterns of sin, immorality, and debauchery? This could indicate that past generations sold out their books of destiny, as they are living without restraint. Write down any common traits you recognize.

_____

_____

_____

_____

_____

_____

_____

# PRAYER

Recognize and renounce these areas. Specifically ask the Lord to **retrieve your book of destiny/ the book of destiny for your family line.** Remember, the Lord wants to restore to you *all* that has been consumed by the enemy!

# OPENING YOUR BOOK OF DESTINY

*For you this whole vision is nothing but words sealed in a scroll.*
*And if you give the scroll to someone who can read, and say, "Read*
*this, please," they will answer, "I can't; it is sealed."*
—ISAIAH 29:11 NIV

The second problem to solve is if you have your book but it isn't open. When you read through Scripture, you'll find that some books were open and some were closed. We'll get to this in just a moment. For instance, Revelation 5 says *the book was sealed*. In the book of Daniel, it says to *seal the book. The time is not yet*. And there are other places where books are open. So it's possible for you to have your book, but your book may not be open.

Here's how you'll know if you have your book but it is closed:

**YOU HAVE A SENSE OF DESTINY BUT YOU DON'T KNOW SPECIFICS AND IT FRUSTRATES YOU; YOU HAVE NO REAL SPECIFICS OF WHAT YOUR DESTINY IS.**

That's because you have possession of your book in the spirit realm, but the book is closed. Therefore, you can't say, "This is who I am and this is what I'm supposed to be doing."

Perhaps you feel that way? Most people do. It is vital to get your book and open it. Why should you open your book? Because you can't go to court without your book. It's impossible to enter the courts of Heaven and present your case without first having your book because, as it says in the Bible, *"The court was seated, and the books were opened."* You're going to present your case from your book. If you don't have your book, you can't present a case.

# OPENING YOUR BOOK

We must retrieve the book, then open it if it is closed. Isaiah 29:10 (NIV) goes on to say something very important: *"The Lord has brought over you a deep sleep: he has sealed your eyes (the prophets); he has covered your heads (the seers)."*

There's a spirit of slumber that has come on you because the prophets' eyes are closed and the seers' heads are covered so they can't see. He's saying the spirit of slumber is the result of no prophetic revelation. In other words, where there is no prophetic revelation, the people will slumber. Those in this state have an *awareness* of destiny, but no proactivity in moving toward fulfillment. It's available, but elusive. You've got to have prophetic revelation moving in the midst of the people. Without prophetic revelation moving, a spirit of slumber will come because it's the prophetic word that keeps us alive and pulsating and moving forward and excited about God and life.

Prophetic revelation births vision. In the next verse, Isaiah tells us why there is no prophetic revelation:

> *For you this whole vision is nothing but words sealed in a scroll. And if you give the scroll to someone who can read, and say, "Read this, please," they will answer, "I can't; it is sealed"* (Isaiah 29:11 NIV).

There is no prophetic revelation, the prophets can't see, and the seers have no perception because the book is *sealed*. There is a book in the spirit realm that's sealed. This is why if a prophet comes to your church or ministry and walks before a line of people and prophesies to everybody except a few, it could be that God wants that few to hear Him for themselves, or it could be that their books are not open.

**PROPHETS CAN ONLY PROPHESY FROM OPEN BOOKS.**

Because prophets can only prophesy from open books, if you haven't done what needs to be done to get your book open, they can't give you a prophetic word. They might be nice and courteous and just say some nice things to you, but they're not going to give you a word of destiny because they can only prophesy from open books.

We must open our books in Heaven. Churches need to open the books. Businesses need to open the books. Cities need to open the books. The Church needs to open the books of cities and nations to prophesy the destinies that affect millions of people. This is the way it works. There was no prophetic understanding because the books were sealed. They couldn't read the scroll, or book, because it was sealed.

In the following entries, you will learn about some powerful tools that will help *open the books of destiny*!

# REFLECTION

Explain the connection between open books and prophetic revelation—why do you think open books are necessary in order for prophets to release prophetic words and decrees?

_____

_____

_____

_____

_____

_____

_____

_____

_____

_____

_____

_____

_____

_____

_____

_____

_____

_____

_____

_____

_____

_____

_____

_____

# TRUE WORSHIP AND TIMING

*The Lord says: "These people come near to me with their mouth and honor me with their lips, but their hearts are far from me. Their worship of me is based on merely human rules they have been taught."*
—ISAIAH 29:13 NIV

First, we must retrieve our book. Second, we need to open it if it is closed. There are five steps or principles to open your book: 1) true worship, 2) timing, 3) tears of intercession, 4) the right basis, and 5) apostolic decrees and authority.

Today, you will review the first two—*true worship* and *timing*.

## NUMBER 1: TRUE WORSHIP

The reason the books were sealed is because there was no true worship. They were "reading the words off the screen"—as many do nowadays—but their hearts weren't attached to them. Why was there no true worship? There was only false worship, no real worship, which causes books to be closed. On the other hand, *true worship opens books*.

Now stop and think about this. During a true worship service today, many people receive prophetic revelation because in the atmosphere of worship books start popping open. Scrolls start opening and all of a sudden people who don't normally prophesy can prophesy. People who can prophesy go to another level.

> **IN THAT ATMOSPHERE OF WORSHIP, BOOKS ARE OPENING IN THE SPIRIT REALM AND THE PROPHETIC REVELATION OF GOD BEGINS TO MOVE AND FLOW..**

Books are opening. We may not have used those words before, but that's what's happening in the spirit realm. Scrolls are opening. If our eyes could be opened, we would see the atmosphere of Heaven filled with books and scrolls. One night I had a dream that I was fighting for a book. When I awoke, I thought, *What are we fighting for? We're fighting for a book.* We need to fight; there's a book to fight for in your family, your school, church, community, nation, etc. We're fighting for the book that has the destiny of your city and nation in it.

God says, "I want my ecclesia to secure this book." When it's retrieved and opened, then all of a sudden the prophets and the seers can discover and release the destiny and the purpose of that into the courts of Heaven.

## NUMBER 2: TIMING

The second key—timing—is found in Revelation 22:10, *"And he said to me, 'Do not seal the words of the prophecy of this book, for the time is at hand.'"* Don't shut it up. Don't seal it. It's time. Timing opens the book. So what that means to me is that there are some books that, regardless of what we do, are not going to open until it's time. That means when they open and prophetic revelation comes, it is a sign to us that the time has shifted—that it's now time to take a step of faith and move into the next season, into the next arena.

How do we know when it's the next season and now time to take that next step? Because a book has opened with new dimensions of revelation. Now here's the problem:

> **BOOKS CAN OPEN WITH REVELATION,**
> **BUT IF THERE ARE NO PEOPLE OF FAITH**
> **TO MOVE INTO THEM, THEY'RE LOST.**

## REFLECTION QUESTIONS

Describe how the following have the ability to open the books of Heaven:

1. True worship (Isaiah 29:10–13):

_____

_____

_____

_____

_____

2. Timing (Revelation 22:10):

# TEARS OF INTERCESSION OPEN BOOKS

*Let the priests, who minister to the Lord, weep between the porch and the altar.*
—JOEL 2:17

In Revelation 5, John is called up into Heaven, and he sees in Heaven a book in the hands of the One who sits on the throne, and it's sealed with seven seals. When he sees the book, he begins to weep because the book is sealed. Why does he weep? He's weeping because he knows that if that book is not opened, the court can't operate, and everything stagnates and is at a standstill. And the enemy will win and his purposes will be done on the earth because it takes the books being opened for Heaven to move.

Heaven cannot move until books are opened. John begins to weep. He weeps because the book is sealed. And then the angel says, *"Do not weep. Behold, the Lion of the tribe of Judah, the Root of David, has prevailed to open the scroll* [book] *and to loose its seven seals."* John continues, *"I looked, and behold, in the midst of the throne...stood a Lamb as though it had been slain"* (Rev. 5:5-6). This passage reveals that:

> ## THE GOVERNMENTAL ROAR OF THE LION ALWAYS COMES OUT OF THE BROKENNESS OF THE LAMB.

I see some people trying to roar as lions before they've identified with the brokenness of the Lamb.

Only when we come to the deep places of brokenness can God say, *I can trust you with My governmental authority.* The angel said, *Don't weep, the Lion of the Tribe of Judah has prevailed.* But notice it was John's tears connected to the finished works of Jesus, which is what the Lion and the Lamb speaks of. The finished works of Jesus opened the book.

If you want to open books of Heaven, it will cost you tears of intercession. This is why there must be intercessors who weep between the porch and the altar and say, "Lord, spare Your people." Believe me, in America I am weeping between the porch and the altar. Weep for what's written in the books of Heaven for America, Israel, and the world as a whole. Weep for what's written in the books for your nation! God wants intercessors who will weep between the porch and the altar as Joel said, until all of His books for us are retrieved and opened.

On a personal level, how long has it been since you wept over your own destiny? Are you ready now to, under Holy Spirit unction, weep until the book of your destiny opens and God gives you understanding? Here's the issue. Stop chasing somebody to prophesy it to you; rather, set your face toward God in passion and intercede before Him until the book opens. I promise you that once the book is open, you won't have to chase the prophetic—it will find you because your book is open. Anybody can prophesy from it now because the book is open. Tears of intercession open books.

## REFLECTION

Explain how tears of intercession can open books of destiny.

_____

_____

_____

_____

_____

_____

_____

_____

_____

_____

_____

_____

_____

_____

_____

_____

_____

What does it look like to weep in a place of intercession on behalf of your destiny? The destinies of your family members, cities, regions, nations, etc.?

_____

_____

_____

_____

_____

_____

_____

_____

_____

_____

_____

_____

_____

_____

_____

_____

_____

_____

_____

_____

_____

_____

Ask the Holy Spirit to break your heart for the things that break the heart of God—it's out of this place of brokenness that intercession springs forth that opens books of destiny.

# PRESENTING YOUR CASE ON THE BASIS OF GOD'S PURPOSE

*Turn from Your fierce wrath, and relent from this harm to Your people. Remember Abraham, Isaac, and Israel, Your servants, to whom You swore by Your own self, and said to them, "I will multiply your descendants as the stars of heaven; and all this land that I have spoken of I give to your descendants, and they shall inherit it forever."*
—Exodus 32:12-13

Daniel 7:10 says, *"The court was seated, and the books were opened."* Something about the court coming to order opens books. That's what the Bible says. So, if you want books opened, you have to know how, in proper protocol and order, to move into the courts of Heaven and take your place. You have to know how to present cases before the court.

> **MOST OF US PRESENT CASES BASED ON OUR NEED. BUT GOD SAYS TO PRESENT CASES BASED ON HIS PURPOSE.**

The books don't have to be open for you to present cases on the basis of need. You just tell Him what you need. You do that before the Father, as you studied earlier in this course. But you present cases before the court based on His purpose. This is hugely important to understand.

When God told Moses to go away from the people Israel because He was going to wipe them out, Moses presented a case before the Lord saying that He needed to first remove His people and remember His purpose for them. He reminded the Lord that His name is in them; and if He wiped them out, others would mockingly say that God could bring them out but He couldn't bring them in. And God would be accused of being a covenant breaker because He did not keep His word with Abraham, Isaac, and Jacob (see Exod. 32:9–14).

Never once did Moses mention Israel's needs. He talked to God about God's purpose and interest in Israel; and God, on the basis of that petition, spared them. God did so because Moses knew how to make a case before God on the basis of purpose, not need.

If you want the books to open, if you want to get results in the courts, stop presenting your cases on the basis of need. That's what you do before the Father. Come on the basis of His purpose.

You may ask, "Well, wait a minute. What about my kids? Lord, these kids, they've got books in Heaven about them. I need You to move in their behalf, or Your purpose for them is going to be lost. What You intended for them is going to be lost."

We need to quit whining to God about our need and start coming to God based on His purpose. When Moses and others in the Bible went before God on the basis of purpose, books opened! Even after years of presenting cases, I'm still learning how to more and more approach Him on the basis of purpose and say, "God, if You don't move here, Your interest in this matter is going to be lost. Your purpose in this situation is going to be lost."

Nothing is wrong with appealing to Him on the basis of need; we do have that right, but I'm saying in the courts it's about His purpose. And when we come on the basis of His purpose, the courts open!

# REFLECTION

Describe the difference between approaching God based on our need and based on His purpose.

# APOSTOLIC DECREES AND AUTHORITY

*Clearly you are an epistle of Christ, ministered by us, written not with ink but by the*
*Spirit of the living God, not on tablets of stone but on tablets of flesh, that is, of the heart.*
—2 CORINTHIANS 3:3

The apostle Paul was telling the Corinthians, "We haven't written about Jesus on a piece of paper with ink. We've actually, as apostles, written on your hearts about Him. You are our epistles. We have written on your hearts." I believe Paul only wrote on their hearts what was consistent with what was already written about them in Heaven. If he wrote something different from what was written in the books of Heaven about them, he would have caused division.

That means that apostolic decrees and authority open books. Whenever apostles make decrees out of the authority God has given them, books will open. Books can begin to break open on a new level, and all of a sudden revelations come that might not have otherwise because apostolic writing on the heart is in agreement with what's written in the books of Heaven.

## GOD'S HEART IS TO OPEN YOUR BOOKS!

God wants to open our books. He also wants us to retrieve any book we've lost. He wants to open our books so that what's written in the books of Heaven can begin to be revealed. When that happens, we're ready to present cases in the courts of Heaven.

In Isaiah 43:25-26, God says:

> I, even I, am he who blots out your transgressions, for my own sake, and remembers your
> sins no more. Review the past for me, let us argue the matter together; state the case for your
> innocence (NIV).

*"Review the past for me"*—what does that mean? Tell me what I said about you in your book. You see, when we prophesy, pray, petition, decree from the books of Heaven, we are presenting cases in the courts of Heaven. We're saying, "Lord, You said this about me. You said this about my family. This is what You said, Lord, and it has not happened yet. We're bringing this case to You. We're bringing

it based on the prophetic understanding, the prophetic purpose that You spoke concerning a city, a nation, a prophet. Lord, we're bringing this case before You and we're petitioning You on the basis of what You have spoken."

Now you're presenting a case to the courts of Heaven. What happens when you present a case? The accuser's going to give God reasons why you can't have what you're asking for. Then we must take the blood of Jesus and answer every accusation so what God has set in place for us can be freely released in the fullness of what He wrote about us before time began.

# REFLECTION

Explain your understanding of what "apostolic decrees" are and how they have the ability to open books in Heaven.

_____

_____

_____

_____

_____

_____

_____

_____

_____

_____

_____

_____

_____

_____

_____

_____

_____

_____

_____

# PRAYER TO RETRIEVE AND OPEN BOOKS OF DESTINY

I encourage you to use the following prayer as a reference tool when approaching the courts of Heaven to retrieve and open books of destiny.

*Lord Jesus, I want to thank You today that there's a book in Heaven about me. There's a book in Heaven about my family, and I'm saying to You that I want my book. If there is anything controlling or possessing my book, please help me to regain control and possession. I want my book. I want everything that I am to have, everything that You have prepared for me to fulfill and walk in. Everything that pertains to life and godliness.*

*If the enemy and demonic powers through covenants with anything in my bloodline have taken possession of my book, I want it back. So, I say right now that I repent for myself and the sins of my ancestors and any agreement that they made with demonic powers. I ask for the blood to speak in the name of Jesus on my behalf and annul every right of demonic powers to hold my book captive. I'm asking, Lord, for those contracts and those covenants to now be annulled and my book to be let go from demonic powers that would be holding it. I renounce every agreement. I repent of every contract, and I ask, Lord, for the annulling of these things right now by the blood of Jesus. Thank You, Lord.*

*Now, Father, I ask for the angels to be released to retrieve my books, my personal book and the book of my family. I'm asking, Lord, for angelic powers to be released, to grab hold of my book and to bring it to me so that I can possess my book, my family's book that is filled with destiny and filled with purpose. Lord, I want to know my destiny written in the books of Heaven about me and about my family.*

*I am so sorry for anything I have done that has agreed with demonic powers. I am sorry for those agreements, and I ask that each is completely removed, completely revoked and taken out of the way by and through the blood of Jesus and that my book would be let go, even now, and I can have it back. I can have it now so all the years that were eaten up by devouring forces that the productivity of those years would be restored to me and to my family line and the chaos that has resulted because we did not have our book, that restoration would come to us and to our family line from this day forward.*

*I ask You for this, Lord, in Jesus' name. Now, Lord, let the angels bring me my book and our book even as a family, in Jesus' name.*

Focus on the Lord for just another moment as you pray:

*Father, I ask that the angelic powers of Heaven bring my book to me, the scroll from Heaven. Anything that's been lost, anything that's been taken captive, let it now come back to me, Lord. Even now, Lord Jesus. I'm sorry for not stewarding my book, for taking it for granted, for not treating rightly the destiny and the purposes of God. I'm sorry for these things, Lord. I'm asking now for these things to be released and opened, Lord, even now, Lord Jesus. Thank You for Your kindness, Holy Spirit. Angels, come. Bring the book to me. Everything that's been lost, all the desolation of many generations. Let the book be restored, Lord. Thank You for doing this for me, Lord. Hallelujah!*

After sincerely praying that prayer, I believe that you may see an angel coming with your book. Or you may actually feel the weight of a book in your hands. This is what happens whenever I ask people after praying this prayer. They literally see their books being restored, and they sometimes feel the weight of the books coming into their hands.

Can more than one book be restored? Yes. There may have been premature deaths in your family line, and those were destinies not fulfilled. So not only will your personal destiny be restored, but also the destiny of the family line that's being restored. God wants to fulfill those destinies in the generations to come.

*I'm declaring a restoration of destiny over you—a sense of destiny that will overtake you. What has been lost and has caused all sorts of heartache and pain because of sexual immoralities, divorce, sicknesses, illnesses, addictions, all these things that were the result of having no vision. I say right now that is broken off you and off your family line. You shall have a sense of destiny and a sense of purpose that you will begin to fulfill in Jesus' name.*

# Session 6

# AN INTRODUCTION TO CURSES

One of the enemy's strategies against believers is to try and keep them from reaching and living their God-given destinies. He does this by presenting a legal case against them. That's what he sought to do with Peter, because if Peter lived his destiny he would push forward the purposes of God on a great level in a great way. It's the same way with us. If we fulfill our destiny in God, we will push the purposes of God forward and God's will shall be done on earth!

First Peter 5:8 says, *"Be sober, be vigilant; because your adversary the devil walks about like a roaring lion, seeking whom he may devour."* The evil one brings lawsuits and builds cases against us to have a legal right to devour us—our futures, purposes, anything he can possibly devour. Anytime I start sensing or feeling something like that coming against me, I try to figure out the legal issue that the enemy may be using to accomplish his fiendish plan.

This session is an introduction to the main strategy the adversary uses to find legal rights of entry into our lives and family lines—*curses*.

## SUMMARY

Curses are what the adversary uses to prevent people from fulfilling destiny. Usually, the context of curses—generational and otherwise—deals with issues of the past and issues of the present. Past alignments, sins, or iniquities have introduced curses into family lines and have thus created a "present reality" filled with torment and oppression by the enemy. Likewise, curses are not just obtained through the bloodline but also through sinful agreements that provide the enemy open access to "land" curses on our lives. The higher demonic objective of curses is this: to prevent you from fulfilling your destiny.

The devil doesn't merely use curses to introduce torment or hardship into your life, although those are the immediate results. His greater goal is to use those curses to restrain you from fulfilling what's written in your book of destiny. Curses are directly aimed at what's written in your book.

In many circles, the subject of "curses" can be controversial. On one end of the extreme, there are theological perspectives that insist the redemptive work of Jesus completely dealt with the possibility of curses and thereby rendered it impossible for believers, cleansed by Jesus' blood and filled with the Spirit, to have curses "land" on them. There is validity in this perspective in that Jesus' atoning work on the cross completely and eternally broke the power of every curse. The other perspective, unfortunately, places an exaggerated emphasis on curses, to the point where everything and anything you might do, say, or participate in could open you up to be possibility of being cursed.

*What is the Bible balance?* In both the video session and through this interactive manual, you will discover how curses are very much a reality. Likewise, you will discover how the work of Jesus completely destroyed the power of every curse. The key to dissolving curses in your life is executing the verdict of the cross. While the cross rendered certain legal verdicts, these verdicts must be appropriated and executed by believers in order for the provisions of Calvary to be made manifest.

# INTERACTIVE QUESTIONS

1. Read Proverbs 26:2.

   *Like a flitting sparrow, like a flying swallow, so a curse without cause shall not alight* (Proverbs 26:2).

   What does it mean for curses to "alight" or *land* on someone?

   _____

   _____

   _____

   Can curses just randomly land on *anyone*?

   _____

   _____

   _____

   _____

2.  Read Galatians 3:13 and Revelation 22:3.

    *Christ has redeemed us from the curse of the law, having become a curse for us* (for it is written, "Cursed is everyone who hangs on a tree") (Galatians 3:13).

    *And there shall be no more curse, but the throne of God and of the Lamb shall be in it, and His servants shall serve Him* (Revelation 22:3).

    Explain your understanding, based on Scripture, of how people can receive curses even when Jesus *became* a curse for us through the cross.

    _____

    _____

    _____

    _____

    _____

    _____

---

**THE WORK OF CHRIST MADE LEGAL
*PROVISION* TO DEAL WITH CURSES.**

---

3.  Describe the legal transaction of the cross. What does it mean to execute the verdicts of the cross in your life?

    _____

    _____

    _____

    _____

    _____

4.  What are some of the "verdicts" that the cross made available that need to be executed and appropriated by believers in order for them to be made manifest?

    _____

    _____

    _____

_____

_____

_____

_____

_____

5. What are curses the result of?

_____

_____

_____

_____

_____

_____

_____

6. Read Ezekiel 18:2-3.

   _"What do you mean when you use this proverb concerning the land of Israel, saying: 'The fathers have eaten sour grapes, and the children's teeth are set on edge'? As I live," says the Lord God, "you shall no longer use this proverb in Israel"_ (Ezekiel 18:2-3).

   How does this Scripture reveal the _will and intent_ of God concerning generational curses?

_____

_____

_____

_____

_____

_____

7. Read Ezekiel 18:30.

   _"Therefore I will judge you, O house of Israel, every one according to his ways," says the Lord God. "Repent, and turn from all your transgressions, so that iniquity will not be your ruin"_ (Ezekiel 18:30).

Explain how this verse fits in the context of Ezekiel 18:2-3. Describe how it is possible for God to have a perfect will and intent that does *not* get fulfilled because of transgression (that opens doors for curses)?

_____
_____
_____
_____
_____
_____
_____
_____
_____

> ## CURSES ARE THE RESULT OF THE ENEMY
> ## HAVING DISCOVERED A LEGAL RIGHT
> ## TO OPERATE AGAINST US.

8. In reflection, discuss how it's possible for God to have a perfect will and intent—that people would live *without curses*—and yet people continue to open doors for curses to land upon their lives.

_____
_____
_____
_____
_____
_____
_____
_____

9. Read Numbers 22:6.

*Therefore please come at once, curse this people for me, for they are too mighty for me. Perhaps I shall be able to defeat them and drive them out of the land, for I know that he whom you bless is blessed, and he whom you curse is cursed* (Numbers 22:6)

What is one of the key purposes of curses?

_____

_____

_____

_____

_____

_____

_____

_____

_____

_____

_____

_____

_____

_____

_____

**A LEGAL RIGHT IS WHAT GIVES A CURSE THE OPPORTUNITY TO LAND IN OUR LIVES.**

# ACTIVATION EXERCISE: DEFINING THE CURSES THAT ARE AIMED AT YOUR DESTINY!

Due to the level of controversy and confusion surrounding curses, it's important for you to articulate what you believe, based on what Scripture says.

Using the manual and video sessions as a guide, look up the following Scripture passages about curses. You might have interacted with some of these already as you've worked through the interactive manual. In order for you to dissolve the curses aimed at your destiny, the first thing you need to have is a basic understanding what curses are and how they operate. Many believers remain disconnected from this reality due to imbalanced or negligent teaching on the subject matter.

Read the following Scriptures. Write down your observations and reflections in the space provided below:

Proverbs 26:2:

Galatians 3:13:

Revelation 22:3:

Ezekiel 18:2-3, 30:

Numbers 22:6:

Based on what you read in Scripture, and you have studied in this session, articulate your understanding of what curses are and how they operate:

# DO CURSES STILL EXIST IN THE NEW COVENANT?

*Like a flitting sparrow, like a flying swallow, so a curse without cause shall not alight.*
—**PROVERBS 26:2**

A curse has to have a cause to affect a person. So, when the Bible says a "cause," that means a legal right. The cause of a curse has been discovered in the spirit realm that allows the curse to land and disrupt a person's destiny.

Some people believe that because we're in the New Testament era, curses don't exist anymore. I would like that to be true, but I know differently. People believe that curses do not exist anymore because Jesus took care of that when He died on the cross. I want to discuss my views on this subject before we proceed.

> **WHEN JESUS DIED ON THE CROSS, EVERYTHING LEGAL THAT NEEDED TO BE DONE TO DEAL WITH CURSES AND TO BREAK CURSES WAS ACCOMPLISHED. BUT THE VERDICT THAT WAS RENDERED HAS TO BE EXECUTED INTO PLACE, AND WE HAVE BEEN EXECUTING THE VERDICT OF THE CROSS FOR 2,000 YEARS.**

First of all, in the New Testament we read in Galatians 3:13 that *"Christ has redeemed us from the curse of the law, having become a curse for us."* So because Jesus became a curse for us, the reality of having to live under the demonic torment of curses is no longer applicable for our lives—*I say yes and amen*. I believe that with every fiber of my being. I believe that when Jesus died on the cross, He *did* become a curse and He dealt with curses. But here's the issue. He dealt with it, but Revelation 22:3

says that in the millennial reign of Christ, there *"shall be no more curse."* So how do we reconcile these two seeming contradictions?

We're still executing it into place because when there is a new Heaven and a new earth, there will be a full manifestation of the verdict of the cross so there is no more curse that can affect the earth or touch the world—the cross will then be in full effect functionally.

Some people still say, "Wait a minute, when Jesus died, all that was accomplished." My reply—I believe that; but if that is true, if it's automatic, then the moment someone gets saved and accepts Jesus as Savior, the person ought to be instantly healed—but that is not usually the case. Why? Because the verdict has to be in place to become a reality. I'm not denying that Jesus did it all, that Jesus paid for it all, and that curses were dealt with when Jesus died on the cross and was raised from the dead. I'm saying that a legal verdict was rendered, but that it has to be executed into place for it to become reality.

# BIBLE STUDY

Reflect on Proverbs 26:2. Explain how a curse finds a "legal right" of entry into our lives. This would be the *curse with a cause.*

# REFLECTION

Explain what it means to execute the legal verdicts of the cross (for example, Jesus *became a curse*, but we still have to execute the provision that was made available through the cross).

# CAN CURSES BE PASSED ON GENERATIONALLY?

*"Why do people use this proverb about the land of Israel: The
children are punished for their fathers' sins? As I live," says the Lord
God, "you will not use this proverb anymore in Israel."*
—EZEKIEL 18:2-3 TLB

People say that because of this verse there is no such thing as the sin of the fathers—sins of previous generations—affecting us now. That's exactly what it *does* say. Their fathers committed some kind of sin, iniquity, and its effect is now touching the children. The declared intent of God is that He does not want the sin of the fathers (ancestors) affecting the lives of future children. He does not want the enemy to be able to use the sins of the fathers as problems for future generations. So, He's saying, "I don't want you using this proverb because I want to do away with this, but you're going to have to cooperate with Me."

The key comes at the end of Ezekiel 18:

> *"Therefore I will judge you, O house of Israel, every one according to his ways," says the Lord God. "Repent, and turn from all your transgressions, so that iniquity will not be your ruin"* (Ezekiel 18:30).

Ezekiel is saying that the intent of God is for the sin of the fathers not to affect the children, but in order to get that promise you have to repent. Because if you don't repent of your transgression and your agreement with iniquity, the iniquity of the fathers will be your ruin.

God is saying to us that this is His intent, but to get that promise we have to grab hold of the process—repent of transgressions and iniquities and declare to Him that we don't want anything to destroy our future and destiny.

In the New Testament it says Jesus dealt with the curse on the cross, and yet there will be no more curse in the millennial reign of Christ. But up until that time, what are we doing? We're daily dealing with the issues of iniquity. We're dealing with the issues of sin in the bloodline that the enemy legally uses to try to stop us. He continually brings curses against us and hinders us from reaching the destiny God has for us.

This is why we are frustrated. We have an intuitive sense from the books of Heaven that we have a God-given purpose. Remember, this is written on our hearts! We have an intuitive sense that we were made for something more than what we're actually living out.

You may have that sense right now. Remember, God's going to move us into more, but to get that we have to deal with the legal case against us in the courts of Heaven that allows curses to land on us and try to stop us from fulfilling the destiny God has for us.

## REFLECTION

Explain how God can have a will and intent that is different than what happens in reality. For example, God's will and intent in Ezekiel 18 was that curses would not continue to be passed on to future generations. His will was that the proverb, *"The children are punished for their fathers' sins"* would not be used anymore in Israel. However, it still continued to take place.

How do you make sense of this?

# THE PURPOSE OF A CURSE

*Therefore please come at once, curse this people for me, for they are too mighty*
*for me. Perhaps I shall be able to defeat them and drive them out of the land, for*
*I know that he whom you bless is blessed, and he whom you curse is cursed.*
—NUMBERS 22:6

Curses are a result of the enemy having discovered a legal right to operate against us. What's his objective? Weaken us so we can be defeated. This is what we see in the passage from Numbers where Balaam was hired to curse the Israelites.

If the enemy can get a curse operating against us and our family line, we can be defeated. The Lord wants us to know how to go into the courts of Heaven and deal with the legal issue that's allowing a curse to continue so the curse can be dissolved and we can come fully into the future that God has for us.

God wants to move us into the dimension of the courts. Because a curse without a cause cannot land, anything that *does* land is because there is a legal right for it to land. Knowing that, it is critical to know some of the common landing places for curses—not just in your life but also in your blood-line. We will be studying these *landing places* extensively in the next two sessions. There may be some situations we can't seem to break out of to get into our destiny. This may be nothing we have done, but something in our bloodline that has been done that is giving the enemy a legal right to prevent us from coming into the fullness of God's destiny for us.

Let me give you a personal example. My whole life I have had to fight for everything. I had to fight tooth and toenail, and I can't tell you how many promises were broken. It got to the point that I didn't believe anything anybody told me because I just assumed it wasn't going to happen anyway. I literally became a pessimist. I became a skeptic. When I would get my hopes up, they'd be dashed. I was so tired and weary of it all. In the middle of my frustration, when I was ready to cash it all in and forget about my dreams, visions, hopes, or aspirations of having larger realms of influence, I had a dream.

In the dream, there was a present-day judgment against me in a court because my great-grandfather had, through negligence, injured someone. Because of his negligence, there was now a present-day judgment against me. When I was half-awake from that very realistic dream, I thought, *Lord, is there really a court action against me? A natural court action?* When I awoke fully, I realized it was a dream and I knew God was telling me, "Look, the reason these broken promises keep occurring over and over is because your great-grandfather, through negligence, injured someone—and stole away someone's dreams. Therefore, the enemy has a legal right to keep stealing away your dreams."

So that morning I prayed and repented for being negligent in any area of my life. I especially repented for any negligence in my family and in my bloodline, particularly dealing with my great-grandfather's negligence. I didn't know what he had done; I didn't even know him. I just knew from the dream that's what had happened. As I dealt with that issue God revealed to me, within a matter of a couple of weeks everything began to shift.

Promised opportunities that had not materialized began to materialize. Everything began to come into divine order so that doors of opportunity and doors of influence began to open on a higher level. This was all because I dealt with the realm of negligence that my great-grandfather had walked in that allowed the enemy to steal away my dreams. What made the difference? I dealt with a curse that had a legal right to operate against me.

Sometimes we don't understand why things happen until God shows us. You don't need to have special gifts or do anything extraordinary to convince God to do this for you. If you get hungry enough for God and seek Him, He will unveil the cause of the curse, the case against you. He will show you one way or another as He is very capable of revealing what it is the enemy is using against you.

## REFLECTION

How are curses ultimately aimed at peoples' purpose and destiny?

# Session 7

# COMMON LANDING PLACES
# FOR CURSES: PART 1

Listed in the following two sessions are some common landing places for curses. Some of these places may be new to you; others may spur thoughts that will deepen your spiritual awareness.

## SUMMARY

Curses cannot land upon people without a cause—a legal right that grants permission for the curse to find a resting place in our lives and family lines.

The following two sessions will take you through different ways curses can land and alight upon people's lives. This information is being shared for one purpose—to help dissolve the curses aimed at destiny. Every one of these "open doors" provides curses with access points into our lives and thus gives them legal right to "land" on us and, if not properly dealt with, future generations.

Most likely, the reason we are dealing with some of these curses to begin with is because of gateways that were established through previous generation. Remember, a curse cannot simply arbitrarily land on someone. It has to be granted a legal right.

In the following two sessions, you will learn about how curses are granted legal right to land on your life. Likewise, you will be armed in the activation exercises to break, cancel, and dissolve these curses so you can unlock your destiny from the courts of Heaven.

# INTERACTIVE QUESTIONS

1. Read Genesis 9:5-6.

   *Surely for your lifeblood I will demand a reckoning; from the hand of every beast I will require it, and from the hand of man. From the hand of every man's brother I will require the life of man. "Whoever sheds man's blood, by man his blood shall be shed; for in the image of God He made man"* (Genesis 9:5-6).

   Describe your understanding of *innocent bloodshed*. How can this open a doorway for curses—even if you personally were not responsible for the bloodshed?

   _____

   _____

   _____

   _____

   _____

   _____

   _____

   _____

   _____

   _____

2. Read Genesis 3:17–19.

   *Then to Adam He said, "Because you have heeded the voice of your wife, and have eaten from the tree of which I commanded you, saying, "You shall not eat of it": "Cursed is the ground for your sake; in toil you shall eat of it all the days of your life. Both thorns and thistles it shall bring forth for you, and you shall eat the herb of the field. In the sweat of your face you shall eat bread till you return to the ground, for out of it you were taken; for dust you are, and to dust you shall return"* (Genesis 3:17–19).

   Explain how disobedience to the voice of God can open doors for curses? What were some of the results that Adam experienced due to his disobedience?

   _____

   _____

   _____

   _____

3. Read 2 Samuel 21:1.

   *Now there was a famine in the days of David for three years, year after year; and David inquired of the Lord. And the Lord answered, "It is because of Saul and his bloodthirsty house, because he killed the Gibeonites"* (2 Samuel 21:1).

   Explain how covenant-breaking can create a landing place for curses. How is 2 Samuel 21:1 an example of this?

4. What is one common evidence of covenant-breaking curses in our lives?

5. Read 2 Samuel 12:11–13, where the Lord renders judgment for David's sin with Bathsheba.

   *"Thus says the Lord: 'Behold, I will raise up adversity against you from your own house; and I will take your wives before your eyes and give them to your neighbor, and he shall lie with your wives in the sight of this sun. For you did it secretly, but I will do this thing before all Israel, before the sun.'" So David said to Nathan, "I have sinned against the Lord." And Nathan said to David, "The Lord also has put away your sin; you shall not die"* (2 Samuel 12:11–13).

   Based on this account, how did *two* areas—what David did with Bathsheba and to her husband, Uriah—open doors for distinct curses to land?

   _____

   _____

   _____

   _____

   _____

   _____

6. Read 2 Samuel 12:14.

   *However, because by this deed you have given great occasion to the enemies of the Lord to blaspheme, the child also who is born to you shall surely die* (2 Samuel 12:14).

   Explain your understanding of how God dealt with David's sexual sin with Bathsheba and how He dealt with David's sin of committing innocent bloodshed.

   _____

   _____

   _____

   _____

   _____

   _____

   _____

# ACTIVATION EXERCISE:
# IDENTIFY CURSES THAT MAY HAVE LANDED UPON YOU:
# PART 1

As you work through these next two sessions, it is important that you enter this time of interaction with the Holy Spirit very intentionally.

1.  Ask the Holy Spirit to lead you through the process of identifying curses that might have landed upon your life.

2.  Invite the Holy Spirit to protect you from condemnation from the enemy, as this tends to shut down the process of people evaluating possible open doors to curses. (They give up because they are overwhelmed by the accuser's condemnation.)

3.  Refuse the temptation for intense introspection. Only focus on what the Holy Spirit reveals and highlights to you. Remember, the reason God would make any of these curses known to you is *not* to make you feel bad about them but to give you the ability to repent for these things and renounce their tormenting influence over your life. God reveals curses to you because He wants to break their hold over you. He wants you to execute the judgment of the cross against these curses.

4.  Begin to pray through the list. Reviewing the different classifications of curses that were introduced in this session, begin to pray through them and ask the Holy Spirit to highlight anything that needs to be addressed—in your life or as the result of previous generational iniquities.

Some sample prayers are being provided next to each category of curses, along with space to write down what the Holy Spirit reveals to you.

### Innocent Bloodshed

> *Holy Spirit, shine Your freeing light of conviction on any area of my life/my history where innocent bloodshed has been committed.*

Wait on the Lord and listen for what He says/reveals.

Write what He shares in the space below:

_____

_____

_____

_____

*Father, I repent for and renounce any innocent bloodshed that has been committed through my family line (name, specifically, anything the Holy Spirit brings to your attention and call it out).*

*I execute the verdict of the cross over this right now in Jesus' Name in the place of prayer. I declare that Jesus became a curse on Calvary so I would not have to live under the torment and tyranny of curses in my life.*

*Right now, because of His blood and because of the legal verdicts rendered at the atonement, I ask that any curses that have landed upon my life because of innocent bloodshed be broken in the Name of Jesus. Thank You, Lord!*

*I rebuke and cancel any assignment of premature death in the name of Jesus!*

*Who the Son sets free is free indeed! I receive Your freedom, right now, and thank You that all the tormenting effects are broken. Thank You, Holy Spirit, that books of destiny are being retrieved and opened right now!*

## Disobedience to God's Voice

*Holy Spirit, shine Your freeing light of conviction on any area of my life/my history where there has been a major act of disobedience committed to Your voice.*

Wait on the Lord and listen for what He says/reveals.

Write what He shares in the space below:

*Father, I repent for and renounce my disobedience to Your voice (name, specifically, anything the Holy Spirit brings to your attention and call it out).*

*I also repent for and renounce disobedience to Your voice committed by previous generations.*

*I execute the verdict of the cross over this right now in Jesus' Name in the place of prayer. I declare that Jesus became a curse on Calvary so I would not have to live under the torment and tyranny of curses in my life.*

*I reverse diminished return for my labor, in the Name of Jesus. Where there was lack, I declare increase because the curse has been reversed!*

*Right now, because of His blood and because of the legal verdicts rendered at the atonement, I ask that any curses that have landed upon my life because of disobedience to Your voice be broken in the Name of Jesus. Thank You, Lord!*

*Who the Son sets free is free indeed! I receive Your freedom, right now, and thank You that all of the tormenting effects are broken. Thank You, Holy Spirit, that books of destiny are being retrieved and opened right now!*

*Covenant Breaking*

*Holy Spirit, shine Your freeing light of conviction on any area of my life/my history where I have broken a covenant or others in my family history have broken covenants (perhaps one of the most significant is marriage/divorce).*

Wait on the Lord and listen for what He says/reveals.

Write what He shares in the space below:

_Father, I repent for and renounce any covenants that I have broken (name, specifically, anything the Holy Spirit brings to your attention and call it out)._

_I also repent for and renounce covenants broken by previous generations._

_I execute the verdict of the cross over this right now in Jesus' Name in the place of prayer. I declare that Jesus became a curse on Calvary so I would not have to live under the torment and tyranny of curses in my life._

_I repent for marriages that ended in divorce (either your own or those of previous family members). Thank You, Father, that You are the restorer of the breach. You make all things new, right now, and I ask for the work of the cross to cleanse my bloodline of the effects of broken covenants._

_Right now, because of Jesus' blood and because of the legal verdicts rendered at the atonement, I ask that any curses that have landed upon my life because of broken covenants be broken in the Name of Jesus. Thank You, Lord!_

_Who the Son sets free is free indeed! I receive Your freedom, right now, and thank You that all of the tormenting effects are broken. Thank You, Holy Spirit, that books of destiny are being retrieved and opened right now!_

### Sexual Sin

_Holy Spirit, shine Your freeing light of conviction on any area of my life/my history where I have participated in sexual sin or others in my family history have participated in sexual sin._

Wait on the Lord and listen for what He says/reveals.

Write what He shares in the space below:

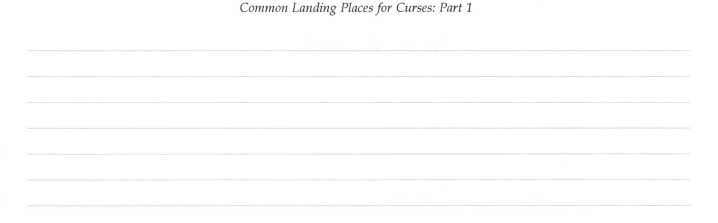

*Father, I repent for and renounce any sexual sins that I have committed directly (name, specifically, anything the Holy Spirit brings to your attention and call it out).*

*I also repent for and renounce sexual sins committed by previous generations (name, specifically, anything the Holy Spirit brings to your attention and call it out).*

*I execute the verdict of the cross over this right now in Jesus' Name in the place of prayer. I declare that Jesus became a curse on Calvary so I would not have to live under the torment and tyranny of curses in my life.*

*I repent for fornication—sexual sins that took place before marriage (premarital sex and sexual acts, pornography, sexual fantasy/imaginations, books, movies, etc.).*

*I repent for adultery—sexual sins that took place in my marriage (sexual affairs, emotional affairs, pornography, etc.).*

*I repent for sexual thoughts and words—fantasies, lustful imaginations, and crude joking/conversation.*

*Right now, because of Jesus' blood and because of the legal verdicts rendered at the atonement, I ask that any curses that have landed upon my life because of sexual immorality and sexual sin be broken in the Name of Jesus. Thank You, Lord!*

*Who the Son sets free is free indeed! I receive Your freedom, right now, and thank You that all of the tormenting effects are broken. Thank You, Holy Spirit, that books of destiny are being retrieved and opened right now!*

# LANDING PLACE 1: INNOCENT BLOODSHED

*And for your lifeblood I will surely demand an accounting. I will demand an accounting from every animal. And from each human being, too, I will demand an accounting for the life of another human being. "Whoever sheds human blood, by humans shall their blood be shed; for in the image of God has God made mankind."*
—GENESIS 9:5-6 NIV

God is saying that whoever sheds innocent blood, whoever kills a person prematurely, that act allows a judgment of premature death to come upon that person and that family line. We scratch our heads, asking, "Why did that happen? Why did that child die prematurely? Why did that young person die so soon? There are not always cut-and-dried answers, but when you understand these principles some things will start to make more sense than they made before. Instead of just scratching our heads and maybe listening to some far-out theology that doesn't make a lick of sense, consider this teaching. *Innocent bloodshed can be the root of premature death.*

For example, one time I was teaching this truth in Missouri, and when I finished the pastor came to me and said, "I have several siblings who died prematurely. It's happened on a regular basis through the years." He said, "We're young people, yet I've had brothers and sisters who have died prematurely." He continued, "When my brother died not too long ago, another brother died. My grandmother came to me and said, 'I need to tell you something that you don't know and nobody else in the family really knows. Your grandfather, when he was a young man, was in a bar fight and he stabbed and killed a man with a knife. And I know that him killing that man with the knife and shedding blood has allowed a curse of premature death to come into our family line.'"

The pastor said to me, "I agreed with my grandmother and told her that we needed to deal with that." Even though the pastor was repentant, the sin of his grandfather and anybody else in the blood-line who was guilty of anything was still allowing premature death to occur. So I tell people that it is a very good practice to say, "Lord, I repent of anything I've been involved with and anything in my bloodline that resulted in innocent bloodshed. I repent so that every legal right of premature death that the enemy would use to execute against me and my family is taken out of the way."

# REFLECTION

Why do you think innocent bloodshed is such an important issue?

# LANDING PLACE 2: DISOBEDIENCE TO GOD'S VOICE

*Then to Adam He said, "Because you have heeded the voice of your wife, and have eaten from the tree of which I commanded you, saying, 'You shall not eat of it': 'Cursed is the ground for your sake; in toil you shall eat of it all the days of your life.'"*
—GENESIS 3:17

In Genesis 3:17–19, God basically says to Adam, "Because you obeyed the voice of your wife rather than the voice of God, you're cursed. You're going to toil, but the ground will bring forth thorns and thistles. It will not bring forth fruitfully." What was the curse on Adam? The curse was diminished returns from his labors. Stop and think about that curse on Adam. Adam would not prosper on the level God intended him to prosper because he chose to listen to the voice of someone other than God, which is idolatry.

If we listen to and obey a voice above the voice of God, we move into a realm of idolatry. So maybe if someone in your bloodline listened to the voice of someone else and stepped into idolatry rather than fully obeying God, that could be the reason why you work so hard but never get ahead. You may be doing everything you know to do, have the right education, the right everything, but it doesn't matter what you do—you never quite get to that next level. Look to the Lord and repent of that for yourself or anyone in your bloodline.

Maybe you can't experience financial breakthrough because the curse of diminished returns is operating against you. So what to do? Pray:

*Lord, I repent for any place that I have or anybody in my bloodline has chosen to listen to another's voice besides You. I repent of this.*

When you pray in this way, you remove the legal right of the enemy to execute a curse against you. You need to understand that the enemy always uses the standard of God against us. In other words, he says, "Lord, Your word says this; therefore, I have a right to do this because this is the penalty for disobedience in this area."

# REFLECTION

Explain the connection between disobedience to God's voice and diminished returns.

# LANDING PLACE 3: BROKEN COVENANTS

*There was a famine in the days of David for three years, year after year;*
*and David inquired of the Lord. And the Lord answered, "It is because of*
*Saul and his bloodthirsty house, because he killed the Gibionites."*
—2 SAMUEL 21:1

Breaking a covenant gives curses a right to land. In essence, God is saying to David, "The reason I haven't been able to answer your prayer to bring rain into the land and break the famine is because the covenant was broken, which gave the enemy a legal right to resist and allow the curse of a famine to land and take hold."

For their prayers for rain to be answered, they would have to deal with the legal issue of the broken covenant. So they had to fix that. Broken covenants can cause famine—famine in families, in finances, in health, etc. In other words, if there is a broken covenant (promise) anywhere in our lives, it can prevent the blessings of God from being received. The devil has a legal right to resist it.

A broken covenant includes divorce. I'm not saying God doesn't forgive, but I'm saying if there's divorce in your family history, you should deal with that in the spirit realm. Maybe it was or wasn't your fault; the issue is if it's in the lineage of your family, the enemy can use that as a legal right.

In the Scripture cited from 2 Samuel, that broken covenant had happened seventy years prior. It wasn't something David had done, yet he suffered the consequences of the broken covenant. You can be suffering the consequences of a broken covenant in your family line because of what happened in someone else's life. You have to repent for yourself and the sins of your ancestors.

If you are experiencing famine on any level, you might want to look into the area of broken covenants. It gives the enemy a legal right to land curses against us that operate. And don't forget, it may not be you. It could be issues in your bloodline that would allow these things to happen.

# REFLECTION

Compile a list of *broken covenants* that could be open doors for curses to land in peoples' lives. This is not something that people think about too often because the word *covenant* is not a common part of modern vocabulary. Still, it is very relevant and should be prayerfully considered.

# LANDING PLACE 4: SEXUAL SIN

*"Behold, I will raise up adversity against you from your own house; and I will take your wives before your eyes and give them to your neighbor, and he shall lie with your wives in the sight of this sun. For you did it secretly, but I will do this thing before all Israel, before the sun."*

*So David said to Nathan, "I have sinned against the Lord." And Nathan said to David, "The Lord also has put away your sin; you shall not die. However, because by this deed you have given great occasion to the enemies of the Lord to blaspheme, the child also who is born to you shall surely die."*
—2 SAMUEL 12:11–14

Sexual sin allows curses a place to land. King David's sin with Bathsheba allowed a curse to land; see the complete unfolding of this tragic story in 2 Samuel 11:2–5; 12:11–14. I've heard my whole life that there's no such thing as big and little sin—as though there were no levels of severity when it came to sin. I agree with that when it comes to forgiveness. God can forgive any and all sin; the blood of Jesus is sufficient for all of us. But the *effects* of sin *do* have big and little consequences, and sexual sin can have huge consequences in family lines. This was especially true for King David.

The Bible says David sinned *in secret*. Secret sins can cause and allow curses to land. David committed a secret sexual sin that allowed a landing place. What was one of the consequences of that sin? His son Absalom would commit fornication and adultery with David's concubine—on the rooftop so everyone would watch; he defiled and disgraced his father.

David also had Uriah, Bathsheba's husband, killed, which was the shedding of innocent blood. So what happened then? Verse 14 says, *"By this deed you have given great occasion to the enemies of the Lord to blaspheme."* He's not talking about the Philistines and the Midianites and all that. Number one, they wouldn't have cared about David having sexual relations with Bathsheba. The *enemies of the Lord* were those in the unseen realm—demonic spiritual forces. When God says you have given the enemy an opportunity to blaspheme, He's saying you have given the unseen forces a right to bring an accusation against you. In other words, this accusation against you will result in a curse and the child that Bath-sheba has will die. The death of the child was the result of David killing Uriah. That allowed the curse of premature death to land on the child, not because of David's sexual sin but because he had Uriah killed to cover it up.

There were two sins and two consequences—sexual sin and murder. The sexual sin—the judgment was Absalom on the rooftop. The murder—the child would die in spite of David crying out to the Lord. Why? The enemies of the Lord, the principalities and powers in the demonic realm, had a right to bring an accusation before the courts of Heaven as the result of David's sexual issues with Bathsheba.

If there are sexual issues in your home life or in your family lines—and by the way there are in most—you need to deal with them. You need to deal with those issues because they give the enemy a legal right to bring all sorts of curses against you. For instance, the Bible cites that those who go into a harlot will be reduced to a piece of bread (see Prov. 6:26). There's all sorts of warnings in Scripture about such things that we don't pay a whole lot of attention to sometimes; but if there are viable sexual issues, you need to say, "Lord, I repent—I repent for the sin in my bloodline that's granting the enemy legal right to bring curses against me and my family and weaken us and stop us from coming into the full destiny that You have for us."

# REFLECTION

Read 1 Corinthians 6:12–20. Why do you think sexual sin comes with such serious and severe consequences?

# Session 8

# COMMON LANDING PLACES FOR CURSES: PART 2

The landing places for curses outlined in the previous session are much more overt and openly recognizable. They can often be easily observed in both our lives and in our family history—innocent bloodshed, sexual sin, disobedience to the voice of God, and breaking covenants.

In this session, you are going to study some of the more *covert* landing places for curses. Even though these are not as blatantly obvious as those previously listed in Session 7, they nevertheless provide equal legal right for curses to land in your life and family line.

## SUMMARY

This session will continue to explore some common landing places for curses. Specifically, you will learn about returning evil for good, curses obtained through authority (abusive authority and rebellion to authority), and finally word curses—where they come from and how you can break them, as these are some of the most common curses that we receive and we release.

## INTERACTIVE QUESTIONS

1. Read Proverbs 17:13.

   *Whoever rewards evil for good, evil will not depart from his house* (Proverbs 17:13).

   How can returning evil for good open doors for curses?

_____
_____
_____
_____
_____
_____
_____
_____
_____

2. Read Micah 2:1–3.

> _Woe to those who devise iniquity, and work out evil on their beds! At morning light they practice it, because it is in the power of their hand. They covet fields and take them by violence, also houses, and seize them. So they oppress a man and his house, a man and his inheritance. Therefore thus says the Lord: "Behold, against this family I am devising disaster, from which you cannot remove your necks; nor shall you walk haughtily, for this is an evil time"_ (Micah 2:1–3).

How can abusive authority open doors for curses?

_____
_____
_____
_____
_____
_____
_____

3. Read Romans 13:2.

> _Therefore whoever resists the authority resists the ordinance of God, and those who resist will bring judgment on themselves_ (Romans 13:2).

How does Paul connect rebellion to judgment/curses?

---

**WHEREVER THERE'S HONOR, THERE'S LIFE.**

---

4. Explain what you understand *word curses* to be and how they operate.

5. Define the two realms of word curses:

   a. Curses that come from the authority you're directly under.

_____

_____

_____

_____

_____

_____

_____

b.   Curses that come from those in place of spiritual authority (but they are not your direct spiritual authority).

_____

_____

_____

_____

_____

_____

_____

_____

_____

_____

_____

**CURSES DON'T STOP UNTIL YOU MAKE THEM STOP.**

6.  Describe the process of breaking word curses over your life.

_____

_____

_____

_____

_____

7. Discussion. What are some ways that you can protect yourself from *speaking* word curses over other people?

8. Discussion. What are some ways that you can protect yourself from *receiving* word curses from other people?

# ACTIVATION EXERCISE:
# IDENTIFY CURSES THAT MAY HAVE
# LANDED UPON YOU: PART 2

As you work through this final session on identifying curses, it is important that you enter this time of interaction with the Holy Spirit very intentionally.

1.  Ask the Holy Spirit to lead you through the process of identifying curses that might have landed upon your life.

2.  Invite the Holy Spirit to protect you from condemnation from the enemy, as this tends to shut down the process of people evaluating possible open doors to curses. (They give up because they are overwhelmed by the accuser's condemnation.)

3.  Refuse the temptation for intense introspection. Only focus on what the Holy Spirit reveals and highlights to you. Remember, the reason God would make any of these curses known to you is *not* to make you feel bad about them but to give you the ability to repent for these things and renounce their tormenting influence over your life. God reveals curses to you because He wants to break their hold over you. He wants you to execute the judgment of the cross against these curses.

4.  Begin to pray through the list. Reviewing the different classifications of curses that were introduced in this session, begin to pray through them and ask the Holy Spirit to highlight anything that needs to be addressed—in your life or as the result of previous generational iniquities.

Some sample prayers are being provided next to each category of curses, along with space to write down what the Holy Spirit reveals to you.

## RETURNING EVIL FOR GOOD

*Holy Spirit, shine Your freeing light of conviction on any area of my life/my history where evil has been returned for good.*

Wait on the Lord and listen for what He says/reveals.

Write what He shares in the space below:

_____

_____

_____

_____

*Father, I repent for and renounce any evil that has been returned for good that has been committed through my family line (name, specifically, anything the Holy Spirit brings to your attention and call it out).*

*I execute the verdict of the cross over this right now in Jesus' Name in the place of prayer. I declare that Jesus became a curse on Calvary so I would not have to live under the torment and tyranny of curses in my life.*

*Right now, because of His blood and because of the legal verdicts rendered at the atonement, I ask that any curses that have landed upon my life because of returning evil for good be broken in the Name of Jesus. Thank You, Lord!*

*Who the Son sets free is free indeed! I receive Your freedom, right now, and thank You that all the tormenting effects are broken. Thank You, Holy Spirit, that books of destiny are being retrieved and opened right now!*

## ABUSING AUTHORITY

*Holy Spirit, shine Your freeing light of conviction on any area of my life/my history where I have used authority to abuse others.*

Wait on the Lord and listen for what He says/reveals.

Write what He shares in the space below:

*Father, I repent for and renounce any abuse of authority that has been committed through my family line (name, specifically, anything the Holy Spirit brings to your attention and call it out).*

*I execute the verdict of the cross over this right now in Jesus' Name in the place of prayer. I declare that Jesus became a curse on Calvary so I would not have to live under the torment and tyranny of curses in my life.*

*I repent for using authority to manipulate others to do what I want them to do.*

*I repent for using authority to control others.*

*I repent for using authority to spiritually manipulate other people.*

*I repent for the sin of witchcraft that is authority abuse.*

*I renounce the controlling spirit of Jezebel and break its hold over my life and previous generations.*

*Right now, because of His blood and because of the legal verdicts rendered at the atonement, I ask that any curses that have landed upon my life because of abuse of authority be broken in the Name of Jesus. Thank You, Lord!*

*Who the Son sets free is free indeed! I receive Your freedom, right now, and thank You that all the tormenting effects are broken. Thank You, Holy Spirit, that books of destiny are being retrieved and opened right now!*

## THE TRAUMA OF ABUSIVE AUTHORITY

*Holy Spirit, shine Your freeing light of conviction on any area of my life/my history where I have experienced abuse by an authority figure (spiritual, teacher, parent, etc.). Thank You, Lord for desiring to break the power and effects of trauma in my life—trauma that opens doors to demonic torment.*

Wait on the Lord and listen for what He says/reveals.

Write what He shares in the space below:

*Father, I repent for and break off the effects of any abuse I have suffered because of authority figures in my life or abuse that previous generations have suffered at the hands of authority figures (name, specifically, anything the Holy Spirit brings to your attention and call it out).*

*I execute the verdict of the cross over this right now in Jesus' Name in the place of prayer. I declare that Jesus became a curse on Calvary so I would not have to live under the torment and tyranny of curses in my life.*

*I repent for unforgiveness and bitterness—my own and that harbored by previous generations.*

*I release my abusers now in the Name of Jesus. As an act of the will, empowered by the Holy Spirit, I set them free from my judgment and my unforgiveness.*

*I break off the effects of abuse and I rebuke the spirit of trauma in the name of Jesus.*

*I break off the effects that memories of abuse have caused in my life, which have given open doors to demonic torment.*

*Right now, because of His blood and because of the legal verdicts rendered at the atonement, I ask that any curses that have landed upon my life because of abuse be broken in the Name of Jesus. Thank You, Lord!*

*Who the Son sets free is free indeed! I receive Your freedom, right now, and thank You that all the tormenting effects are broken. Thank You, Holy Spirit, that books of destiny are being retrieved and opened right now!*

Note: when receiving healing from the trauma produced by abusive authority, it is recommended that you prayerfully consider counseling to help undo effects of this abuse due to the severe and sensitive nature of this. Also, when going through the process of releasing forgiveness to others, it is recommended that you use John and Carol Arnott's book, *Grace and Forgiveness* as a resource (Toronto, ON: Catch the Fire Books, 2015).

# NOT SUBMITTING TO AUTHORITY

*Holy Spirit, shine Your freeing light of conviction on any area of my life/my history where I have not been submissive to authority (godly authority, governmental authority, parental authority, etc.)*

Wait on the Lord and listen for what He says/reveals.

Write what He shares in the space below:

_____

_____

_____

_____

_____

_____

_____

_____

_____

_____

*Father, I repent for and renounce any resistance to godly authority that has been committed through my family line (name, specifically, anything the Holy Spirit brings to your attention and call it out).*

*I execute the verdict of the cross over this right now in Jesus' Name in the place of prayer. I declare that Jesus became a curse on Calvary so I would not have to live under the torment and tyranny of curses in my life.*

*I repent for rebelling against governmental authority.*

*I repent for rebelling against godly authority.*

*I repent for rebelling against parental authority.*

*I acknowledge that the spirit of rebellion is like the spirit of witchcraft, so I break its hold over me right now in the Name of Jesus.*

*In the place of prayer, I go into former generations and break alignment with past rebellion.*

*Rebellion stops here and now—it ends today. I repent for it. I renounce it. I break its power over me and future generation.*

*Right now, because of His blood and because of the legal verdicts rendered at the atonement, I ask that any curses that have landed upon my life because of rebellion be broken in the Name of Jesus. Thank You, Lord!*

*Who the Son sets free is free indeed! I receive Your freedom, right now, and thank You that all the tormenting effects are broken. Thank You, Holy Spirit, that books of destiny are being retrieved and opened right now!*

# BREAKING WORD CURSES

*Holy Spirit, shine Your freeing light of conviction on any area of my life/my history where I have received or released word curses.*

Wait on the Lord and listen for what He says/reveals.
Write what He shares in the space below.

*Word curses you have received from others:*

_____

_____

_____

_____

_____

_____

_____

_____

_____

_____

_____

_____

*Word curses you have released over others:*

_____

_____

_____

_____

_____

_____

_____

_____

_____

_____

_____

_____

_____

*Father, I repent for and renounce any word curses that I have received or released (name, specifically, anything the Holy Spirit brings to your attention and call it out).*

*I execute the verdict of the cross over this right now in Jesus' Name in the place of prayer. I declare that Jesus became a curse on Calvary so I would not have to live under the torment and tyranny of curses in my life.*

*Right now, I undo every word curse that has been brought against me or that I have released over others.*

1.  I repent for every place where I have released a word curse over someone.

2.  Father, I forgive those who have released word curses over me—or over my family/previous generations.

3.  *I speak off the word curses that have landed upon me.* Right now, declare the opposite of the curses that have been released over you. For every curse, declare the blessing of God. Declare reversal. Declare that what was placed upon you through a curse is broken through the power of blessing.

4.  I declare that I let what's written in my book of destiny define me, not word curses from others.

*Right now, because of His blood and because of the legal verdicts rendered at the atonement, I ask that any curses that have landed upon my life because of word curses be broken in the Name of Jesus. Thank You, Lord!*

*Who the Son sets free is free indeed! I receive Your freedom, right now, and thank You that all the tormenting effects are broken. Thank You, Holy Spirit, that books of destiny are being retrieved and opened right now!*

# SESSION NOTES

# LANDING PLACE 5:
# RETURNING EVIL FOR GOOD

*Evil will never leave the house of one who pays back evil for good.*
—PROVERBS 17:13 NIV

If someone does me good and helps me and I turn around and stab him in the back to try to climb higher over them or whatever the case may be, evil will not depart from my house. It doesn't say that evil will necessarily come to me directly, but it will have some effect on my family line.

---

**SOMETIMES WE ARE REAPING THE RESULTS OF WHAT HAS HAPPENED PREVIOUSLY IN OUR FAMILY LINE.**

---

Because someone did evil to someone who did them good, it puts into motion certain consequences. We have to know how to go in and undo those curses because the enemy sees those as legal rights to bring cases against us in the courts of Heaven.

These are some things we have to seriously consider—they are legal issues that allow curses to land in our life or the lives of our family members. Sometimes it looks like people get away with evil actions, but the Bible says, *"Judge nothing before the appointed time"* (1 Cor. 4:5 NIV). If we think they got away with it, we may be judging them prematurely.

Proverbs 17:13 says the person's house will have evil against it. So we have to say, "Lord, for my sake and the sake of my house, anything I've done or anything anybody else has done, I repent of that and ask for the blood of Jesus to speak on my behalf."

# REFLECTION

What are some examples of returning evil for good?

# LANDING PLACE 6: ABUSE OF AUTHORITY

*Woe to those who devise iniquity, and work out evil on their beds! At morning light they practice it, because it is in the power of their hand. They covet fields and take them by violence, also houses, and seize them. So they oppress a man and his house, a man and his inheritance. Therefore thus says the Lord: "Behold, against this family I am devising disaster, from which you cannot remove your necks; nor shall you walk haughtily, for this is an evil time."*
—MICAH 2:1–3

The misuse of authority to bring oppression results in disaster that cannot be removed. Sometimes we search for answers and think, *Why can't I do this or that? Why doesn't it work? Why can't I get ahead? Why can't I come into my destiny?* There may be a curse operating against you and your family line related to something in your history that you simply need to deal with by the blood of Jesus.

Somewhere in your family line—or perhaps, with you—someone used a position or status of authority to control, manipulate, or harm others. As a result of poorly stewarding the authority entrusted to them, they caused a curse to land upon them and, ultimately, their family line. You may or may not be aware of this kind of legal right. While other landing places for curses are much more blatant and easily observable, such as innocent bloodshed and sexual sin, some operate in a much more covert, stealthy manner. The landing places we are observing in this particular session tend to be more "under the radar" outlets for curses to gain a legal right to operate.

So, how can you recognize and repent for a landing place for a curse, such as abuse of authority?

It is wise to say, "Lord, give me any wisdom that I might need to remove a legal curse on me or my family. Speak to me so that I can discern anything that needs to be removed." Remember, this is not deliverance. This is removing barriers, roadblocks, and hindrances out of the way so that we can come forward into the purposes of God. God wants us to reach our destiny. Why? So His purposes can be fulfilled and His will be accomplished on earth.

# REFLECTION

What are some ways that a person can abuse the authority entrusted to him/her by the Lord? It is important for you to consider such a list so you can avoid the temptation to abuse any measure of authority given to you.

## Day 34

# LANDING PLACE 7: REBELLION AGAINST AUTHORITY

*Therefore whoever resists the authority resists the ordinance of God,*
*and those who resist will bring judgment on themselves.*
—ROMANS 13:2

Not only abuse of authority but rebellion against authority can cause curses to land. Why do people rebel against authority? Because they've been wounded by it so often. But if I let my woundedness create lawlessness against authority, it can result in curses landing on me and future generations.

**I CANNOT AFFORD TO ALLOW WOUNDEDNESS TO
GIVE ME A LICENSE TO REBEL AGAINST AUTHORITY.**

I have to submit to authority. I have to honor authority. I have to walk in righteous relationship to authority because the authority that we're under came from God, and if I rebel against that authority, I am in actuality rebelling against God.

We're talking about *righteous* authority here and having a submitted heart. The Lord tells us to honor authority. If we honor, for instance, our father and mother, it will go well with us and our days will be long upon the earth (see Eph. 6:2-3).

**WHEREVER THERE'S HONOR, THERE'S LIFE.**

So anywhere we are in rebellion against authority on any level, we have to repent of that and say, "Lord, please heal me and cleanse me. I don't want to be in rebellion against authority. I want to walk in righteous relationship in and to authority."

## BIBLE STUDY

Read Romans 13:1–7.

## REFLECTION

How are authorities, like those Paul describes in Romans 13:1–7, set up for your protection?

_____

_____

_____

_____

_____

_____

_____

_____

How is resisting *righteous* authority, motivated by a heart of rebellion, the same thing as rebelling against God?

_____

_____

_____

_____

_____

_____

_____

_____

# LANDING PLACE 8: TWO REALMS OF WORD CURSES

*Death and life are in the power of the tongue, and those who love it will eat its fruit.*
—PROVERBS 18:21

The last few entries will focus specifically on the dimensions of *word curses* and how to break them off your life. First, it's important for you to know that there are *two realms of word curses* that you will deal with.

**First Realm: words that come from authority figures who are over you.** This would include your parents, employers, teachers, instructors, mentors, church leaders, etc. If you are under someone's authority and the person speaks evil of you, the enemy takes their words and builds cases in the courts of Heaven. You have to know how to undo those words. Because they are in authority over you, their words can be used to create restrictions against the destiny God has for you.

**Second Realm: words released by those in spiritual authority.** The second realm is connected but different. You may not be under their authority, but if people who have spiritual authority choose to speak against you, their words have the power to curse. If they legitimately have authority in the spirit realm and they don't like something about you and began to speak against you, the enemy takes their words and says in court, "Even those to whom You have given spiritual authority say this about them." Their words have the power to curse.

For example, in 2 Kings 2, Elisha receives the mantle from Elijah. Then Elisha hears the men of the city ask him to *heal the water in Jericho*. Elisha tells them to get some salt and take him to the source of the river. He throws salt into it and decrees: *"Thus says the Lord: 'I have healed this water; from it there shall be no more death or barrenness'"* (2 Kings 2:21). God isn't just healing some bad-tasting water. The word *barrenness* means unable to bear children. *Death* means to die by violence or naturally; so what was happening in the city was premature death occurring because there was a bereavement of children in Jericho.

Why is that significant? Because of the curse that a man of God named Joshua put on that city years prior. When Joshua gave the command to blow the trumpets and shout and the walls fell down in Joshua 6, he cursed the city. He said, *"Cursed be the man before the Lord who rises up and builds this city Jericho; he shall lay its foundation with his firstborn, and with his youngest he shall set up its gates"* (Josh. 6:26). A man named Hiel, in the days of Ahab, rebuilt Jericho and his firstborn and lastborn died (see 1 Kings 16:34). Because Joshua, a man of God who had authority, had spoken a word of curse, death in the city did not stop with Hiel. It continued for generations.

## CURSES DON'T STOP UNTIL YOU MAKE THEM STOP.

This is good news and bad news! If it's a real curse, it's going to keep on, keep on, keep on until someone steps in and breaks the cycle. Deuteronomy 28:45 says, *"Moreover all these curses shall come upon you and pursue and overtake you, until you are destroyed."* Curses are aggressive. Don't think, *Oh, I can outlive this. Things will be better for my next generations.* No, if there's a curse in your family line because of a legal right, it's not going to stop until somebody makes it stop. The encouraging truth is that you have the ability to completely break agreements with curses, causing them to cease and not continue.

Hebrews 13:17 says, *"Obey those who rule over you, and be submissive, for they watch out for your souls, as those who must give account* [someone rightly related to authority]. *Let them do so with joy and not with grief, for that would be unprofitable for you."* The Bible says that if those in authority give an evil report, it will cause grief. If they give an evil report about a person, it can cause the person grief. I say, "Lord, let them speak good!" But even when you've done everything you know to do, sometimes they choose to speak evil anyway, and you have to know how to undo their words.

## REFLECTION

Why do you think words from spiritual authorities carry the ability to curse?

_____

_____

_____

_____

_____

_____

_____

_____

_____

Consider the statement, *Curses don't stop until you make them stop.* Why do you think people willingly live with curses plaguing their lives and then continuing to impact future generations?

# UNDOING WORD CURSES

*"No weapon formed against you shall prosper, and every tongue which rises against you in judgment you shall condemn. This is the heritage of the servants of the Lord, and their righteousness is from Me," says the Lord.*
—ISAIAH 54:17

*"Every tongue which rises against you in judgment you shall condemn."* The word *judgment* means a verdict, so the Lord is saying that people's words can literally be used to sentence us to a destiny not intended for us by God. That's how powerful words can be.

> **IF I DON'T KNOW HOW TO DEAL WITH THEM, SOMEONE'S WORDS CAN CREATE AN ALTERNATE VERSION OF THE LIFE I'M SUPPOSED TO HAVE.**

The word *condemn* means to disturb. It means that I upset the judgment that would work against me. Therefore, I want to share with you four ways you can undo word curses and actually *condemn* the words being spoken against you.

Step 1. First of all **you need to repent for every time you've cursed someone else**. If you have ever cursed someone, if you've ever spoken critically of someone, and if you've ever spoken evil of someone, that in itself is reason for the curses to land. So you have to repent, as best you can, for every time you've cursed someone. Say, *"Lord, I'm sorry for speaking evil of people myself. Out of my own morbid satisfaction, or whatever the motivation, I repent of that, of every instance, and I ask You to forgive me."*

Step 2. Next you have to **forgive those who have cursed you and spoken critically of you**. Now you have to say, *"Lord, please bless those who have cursed me or spoken critically about me. I want their families blessed. I want their lives blessed. I want their ministries blessed. I want them blessed, Lord. I want their* *futures blessed. I don't want evil to come to them. I take no delight in evil happening to them. I want Your blessing on them, God."* Until you can pray that prayer, you haven't really forgiven them.

Step 3. When we have taken care of step 1 and 2, then you **speak those curses out of your life**. Say, *"Lord, let the blood of Jesus right now annul the words spoken against me and remove them from the courts of Heaven so the enemy cannot use them against me anymore."* Now on the other hand, if those words are legitimate and you are guilty of what those words are announcing, you have to deal with some other issues. You have to repent and allow the Holy Spirit to guide you through that. But ultimately, we need to say, *"Lord, let the words be annulled so they have no more power to be used to form a case against me. Let those words be annulled and taken out of the way, out of my life and my family's lives so that the enemy cannot use them to build cases."*

Step 4. Now we say, *"Lord, don't let their words fashion my destiny. Rather, let what's written in the books of Heaven form my destiny. What is in the books of Heaven will determine my destiny, not what somebody else has said."* We need to deal with every issue of word curses and destroy every legal right in the spirit realm so the enemy can't use them to bring a case against us.

# REFLECTION

How can you use this four-step process on a regular basis to protect yourself from the negative impact and effect of word curses?

_____

_____

_____

_____

_____

This is not provided as some kind of religious blueprint or formula; it is literally a process that is intended to help you immediately recognize and cancel the operation of word curses in your life. In fact, word curses might be some of the most prevalent kinds of curses that are routinely released to and through us. With this in mind, it's vital to know how to cancel them as soon as possible before they are given the chance to take root.

# PRAYER FOR BREAKING CURSES

*Lord Jesus, I want to thank You that when You died on the cross You destroyed every right of curses to operate.*

*Lord, may Your blood and Your sacrifice speak for me and my family in the courts of Heaven so that any legal rights of the devil to build cases against us and land curses against us are removed because of who You are, Lord Jesus, and the blood that You have shed for us.*

*Thank You for Your blood that speaks on my behalf and on behalf of my entire family heritage.*

*Thank You, Jesus, that Your blood has the supernatural ability to remove the stain of iniquity and transgression. Your blood has the divine power to go back in time and directly address the landing places where curses were introduced into my family line.*

*Let the curses be dissolved, right now, in Jesus' Name.*

*Lord, let the curse(s) of _____ be dissolved right now so that my destiny can be unlocked and fulfilled.*

*Let them be removed so they can no longer deny my destiny and delay my future.*

*Lord, I come into the fullness of everything that is written about me and my family in the books of Heaven.*

*I come into the fullness of that place because of Your blood, Jesus, and Your grace.*

*Thank You, Lord!*

Isaiah 55:13 says that *"Instead of the thorn shall come up the cypress tree, and instead of the brier shall come up the myrtle tree; and it shall be to the Lord for a name, for an everlasting sign that shall not be cut off."* Let us decree together that every curse is now turned into a blessing, that curses are broken off of our lives and we are able to come into the fullness of everything that God intended.

# Session 9

# UNLOCKING YOUR PROPHETIC SENSES IN THE COURTS OF HEAVEN

## SUMMARY

In order to unlock what's written in your book of destiny, first you need to awaken your prophetic senses. It requires prophetic sight to visualize what is recorded in books of destiny, as it is a supernatural process. This is how prophets and those operating in the gift of prophecy make prophetic observations and declarations. They see glimpses of open books of destiny in the spirit realm and announce what they see.

By going through this concluding session, you will actually enter into the courts of Heaven and ask for prophetic senses to be unlocked.

To move in this realm, you need to recognize that Scripture confirms that all believers can operate in the prophetic. One of the results of the Spirit's outpouring, as outlined in Acts 2, is the prophetic operating in sons and daughters, men and women alike. While there are certain individuals assigned to be prophets in a five-fold ministry context, *all* believers have been given the ability to prophesy.

# INTERACTIVE QUESTIONS

1. Explain the two essential components of entering the courts of Heaven.

    a.   **Faith**: how do you use *faith* to operate in the courts of Heaven?

_____

_____

_____

_____

_____

_____

_____

_____

_____

_____

_____

**FAITH: LEARNING TO BELIEVE WHAT YOU SENSE
AT LEAST AS MUCH AS WHAT YOU SEE.**

    b.   **Functioning in the prophetic realm**: explain why the prophetic is so important to operating in the courts of Heaven.

_____

_____

_____

_____

_____

_____

2. Read 1 Corinthians 14:1–5 in your Bible. Pay close attention to the following passages:

*Pursue love, and desire spiritual gifts, but especially that you may prophesy. For he who speaks in a tongue does not speak to men but to God, for no one understands him; however, in the spirit he speaks mysteries. But he who prophesies speaks edification and exhortation and comfort to men. He who speaks in a tongue edifies himself, but he who prophesies edifies the church. I wish you all spoke with tongues, but even more that you prophesied* (1 Corinthians 14:1–5).

Based on what Paul is explaining to the Corinthian church, describe how it is possible for *all* believers to operate in the spiritual gift of prophecy.

## WE NEED TO ASK FOR THE COURTS OF HEAVEN TO OPEN.

3.  Describe your idea of what it looks like to enter the courts of Heaven. How would you go about doing this based on what you've read in the session/watched in the video?

_____

_____

_____

_____

_____

_____

_____

_____

_____

_____

_____

_____

_____

_____

_____

_____

_____

_____

4.  How can legalistic covenants prevent your prophetic senses from operating? Define what these covenants could look like.

_____

_____

_____

5. Read Revelation 19:10.

   *And I fell at his feet to worship him. But he said to me, "See that you do not do that! I am your fellow servant, and of your brethren who have the testimony of Jesus. Worship God!"* (Revelation 19:10)

   Based on what Robert shares in the video session, *who* is the person John tries to worship? How does this relate to you and your identity in the heavenly realm?

6. Explain why a *prophetic understanding* is important for you to enter the courts of Heaven.

---

**A PROPHETIC UNDERSTANDING: WE HAVE TO READ FROM THE BOOKS OF HEAVEN SO WE CAN PRESENT CASES BEFORE THE COURTS OF HEAVEN.**

---

7. Explain the two agendas of the anti-Christ spirit:

   a. To deny and diminish who Jesus is:

b.  To deny and diminish who you are in Christ:

---

## A PROPHETIC RELEASE: AGREEMENT WITH THE TESTIMONY OF JESUS.

8.  Read Revelation 19:10.

*For the testimony of Jesus is the spirit of prophecy* (Revelation 19:10b).

What does it look like for you to *prophesy* and release what Jesus is *testifying*?

9. Read Hebrews 12:22–24 and Ephesians 2:6.

*But you have come to Mount Zion and to the city of the living God, the heavenly Jerusalem, to an innumerable company of angels, to the general assembly and church of the firstborn who are registered in heaven, to God the Judge of all, to the spirits of just men made perfect, to Jesus the Mediator of the new covenant, and to the blood of sprinkling that speaks better things than that of Abel* (Hebrews 12:22–24).

*And God raised us up with Christ and seated us with him in the heavenly realms in Christ Jesus* (Ephesians 2:6 NIV).

Describe how the description in Hebrews 12:22–24 gives you a spiritual picture of where you *are seated in Christ*—the heavenly realms.

10. How can you use this description to help visualize entering the courts of Heaven?

## A PROPHETIC REALM: THE PLACE WE BEGIN TO OPERATE IN.

# ACTIVATION EXERCISE:
## UNLOCKING YOUR PROPHETIC SENSES IN THE COURTS OF HEAVEN

To start seeing your open book of destiny, you need to have prophetic sight.

Follow the instructions provided by Robert Henderson in Session 9 of the video curriculum. At the conclusion of the session, he will lead you in a prayer that will help usher you into prophetic experiences in the courts of Heaven.

If you do not have immediate access to the video curriculum, you can begin to work through the daily entries and pray through the prayers supplied at the conclusion of this session.

# SESSION NOTES

# YOUR REALM OF JURISDICTION IN THE COURTS OF HEAVEN

*We, however, will not boast beyond measure, but within*
*the limits of the sphere which God appointed us.*
*—2 CORINTHIANS 10:13*

In the courts of Heaven, jurisdiction is very important. Paul used the term *beyond measure* in 2 Corinthians 10:12–17 rather than *jurisdiction*. I use the term *jurisdiction* because it's more familiar, as it is the idea of a sphere of authority, a dimension of authority. Everyone has a measurement of rule for their lives and their family. This was the context that Paul was addressing—specifically his measure of jurisdiction among those he was addressing. In other words, Paul *recognized* and *stewarded* the sphere of authority the Lord had entrusted to him. But when you start dealing with churches and cities and states and nations or whatever it may be, you need to be careful. You pray blessings over all of that; but if you start wrestling with principalities and powers, that's a whole other issue.

If you don't stay within your measurement of rule or your jurisdiction in the courts of Heaven, you open a door for backlash. I do not move outside the realm of jurisdiction that the Lord has given me to function in. I don't assume that I can start taking on things in the spirit that the Holy Spirit has *not* specifically instructed me to or that are outside my measure of jurisdiction. If I'm outside my jurisdiction, I give the enemy a legal right to come after me. I've actually had that happen, and I don't want it to happen ever again. It's not a pleasant thing when the devil has a right to come after you.

For example, sometimes intercessors step into dimensions that they might not have an authority to step into. Just because they are intercessors or even prophetic and can see and sense something in the spiritual realm doesn't mean they have authority to deal with it. If we start taking on principalities and powers, as Paul describes, *"We do not wrestle against flesh and blood, but against principalities, against powers"* (Eph. 6:12), it is possible for us to open doors for the adversary to come against us. I believe Paul was saying that from his apostolic authority God had given him, he had a rank that allowed him and his team, his company, to begin to deal with principalities and powers. I believe we need apostolic authority to be able to deal with the control of regions. Be very careful about realms of jurisdiction when preparing to operate in the courts of Heaven.

As an individual and as part of a family, you have every right to go into the courts of Heaven and deal with issues about your own future, your own destiny, your own inheritance. God wants you to move into these areas, so in this session we will examine how to practically move into those realms and some of the things we need to do there.

# REFLECTION

Why is it important for you to stay within your jurisdiction when operating in the courts of Heaven? How could it be dangerous to start challenging principalities and powers over cities, regions, and nations when, in fact, you have not been directed to take on those assignments?

# ASK FOR THE COURTS OF HEAVEN TO OPEN

*Ask, and it will be given to you; seek, and you will
find; knock, and it will be opened to you.*
—MATTHEW 7:7

In the courts of Heaven, protocol is also very important. The currency of the Kingdom of God is *asking*. We don't demand. We don't simply barge in. We approach the Judge of all the earth with awe and reverence, observing appropriate protocol.

For example, if you are going to present a court case in the natural, you have to get on the docket. You don't just show up one day and say, "Hey, I want to tell you about my case, Judge." We're not dealing with a courtroom in the natural, but it is similar enough that we need to show due honor and due respect for the One we're approaching. I have found it is very helpful to say from a heart of honor, from a spirit of honor, *"Lord, I'm asking You to please open the courts so we can come into the court and have audience with You as the Judge of all, the Righteous Judge."* By faith, you can ask with the expectation that He *will* open the courts for you!

When we come before the Lord as Father and Friend, it's not necessary to announce our intent beforehand. But I believe to respect the protocol of the court, it is proper to speak in advance to the Judge. I didn't always believe that, but the more I have practiced this, the more I have understood that we need to show Him honor and respect—and even walk in the fear of the Lord as we approach Him.

When you actually stand up and ask for the courts to open, that is usually what happens. In fact, even when I'm speaking about this process, I can usually feel the courts open because I feel His hovering presence. Then, we can move into that realm and even ask for things. If you don't feel anything, that's fine—it's not mandatory. With an eye of faith, look around and see what the courts look like. This is why prophetic sight is important when operating in the courts of Heaven. The remaining entries will be focused specifically on helping you unlock your prophetic sight so you can operate in the courts.

It is possible, by faith, to say, "I actually want to learn to focus my prophetic gift so that I am moving and seeing in a certain dimension—the dimensions, Lord, that You are revealing to me." When you learn to do that, you can ask, "Lord, would You please open the courts?" And when we ask, we can step into that place and begin to see from a courtroom perspective.

# REFLECTION

Explain why you believe it's important to use appropriate protocol when entering the courts of Heaven.

Why do you think *asking* the Judge to open the court is necessary? What attitude does it show toward the One you are approaching?

# KEYS TO MOVING IN THE COURTS OF HEAVEN

*But solid food belongs to those who are of full age, that is, those who by reason of use have their senses exercised to discern both good and evil.*
—HEBREWS 5:14

I do not believe the writer of Hebrews is referring to our natural senses in this passage. He's talking about our spiritual senses. That *by reason of using them* we grow in our prophetic senses. Our ability to see, hear, smell, touch, and taste—all these natural senses have a correlating spiritual sense that we can begin to pick up in the unseen world. But here's our problem—we don't realize we're spiritual beings. If we did, God would unlock these new dimensions of the prophetic so that *by reason of use* we can become even more acquainted with that realm and begin to function there.

If you're going to move and function in the spiritual realm of the courts of Heaven, there are two things that are absolutely necessary—faith and the prophetic realm. In other words, you have to move by faith because you're functioning in an unseen world and an unseen realm. You can't put your physical hands on something. You have to be able to believe and say, "Everything I'm going to do I'm going to do by faith."

> **MY DEFINITION FOR FAITH—LEARNING TO BELIEVE WHAT YOU SENSE AT LEAST AS MUCH AS WHAT YOU SEE**

Paul says *"we walk by faith, not by sight"* (2 Cor. 5:7). That means I'm going to live by what I can sense; and if I'm going to function in the unseen realm of the courts of Heaven, I'm going to have to learn how to do that. I'm going to have to learn how to trust and understand those realms.

In the following entries, we will more closely study what it means to function in the prophetic realm and how it is vitally connected to operating in the courts of Heaven.

# REFLECTION

Describe how faith is important to operating in the invisible realm. Specifically, write out what it looks like to use your faith to move in the courts of Heaven.

# First Dimension of Prophetic Sight: Knowing What's in Our Books

*Put me in remembrance; let us contend together; state*
*your case, that you may be acquitted.*
*—Isaiah 43:26*

The first level of the prophetic is *knowing what is in our books of Heaven* so we can present cases in the courts of Heaven. In Isaiah 43:26, the Lord is basically saying: *Tell Me what I wrote about you in the book of Heaven before time began so we can work together to acquit you in the courts of Heaven.*

The only way we can remind God what is in our books is by prophetic understanding. If you're going to perceive what is in your book or in your family's book or whatever you're dealing with, you have to perceive it from prophetic understanding. We're not going to figure it out in the natural. I appreciate spiritual mapping and strategies like that, which can be helpful, but I believe that prophetic understanding is absolutely essential to discerning what is written in the books of Heaven. So, when I present a case in the courts and I'm going to present it based on what's in the books, I have to prophetically perceive that and prophetically understand that.

Because I am very aware of what is written in my book, I can say, "Lord, You said this. You said that." I am speaking and bringing before His courts what I prophetically understand is in my books. You need those kinds of understandings if you're going to present cases. Because again, you're not presenting cases on the basis of need. You're presenting cases on the basis of purpose.

For instance, if I was dealing with an issue, I would say, *"Lord, this thing needs to be fixed because it's hindering Your purpose from coming to pass. Fix this please because it is not consistent with the purpose that You assigned to me and what I'm supposed to be doing."*

## EXERCISE: ACTIVATING THE PROPHETIC

This is the first dimension of the first level of the prophetic. Right now, ask your Father to open your eyes and open your spirit to discern and understand prophetic purpose so that you can present cases in the courts of Heaven.

Reflect and write down what He shares with you.

_____

_____

_____

_____

_____

_____

_____

_____

_____

_____

_____

_____

_____

_____

_____

_____

_____

_____

_____

_____

_____

_____

_____

_____

_____

_____

_____

_____

# SECOND DIMENSION OF PROPHETIC SIGHT: REVELATION IN THE SPIRIT REALM

*At this I fell at his feet to worship him. But he said to me, "Don't do that! I am a fellow servant with you and with your brothers and sisters who hold to the testimony of Jesus. Worship God! For it is the Spirit of prophecy who bears testimony to Jesus."*
—**REVELATION 19:10 NIV**

The first dimension of the prophetic is *receiving revelation in the spirit realm—specifically about our new creation identity in Heaven.* Consider Revelation 19:10 afresh. The apostle John wrote that he "*fell at his feet to worship him.*" Normally we say that John is encountering an angel in Heaven. But you're going to see that this isn't an angel; he is having an encounter in the spirit realm—that's prophetic. He's encountering a heavenly being, but it's not an angel.

There are three reasons it's not an angel:

1. The being said, "*I am a fellow servant.*" That means it was of human origin. An angel is not our "*fellow servant.*"

2. And the being said, "*with you and with your brothers and sisters*" Angels are not our siblings.

3. And then he says, "*Who hold to the testimony of Jesus.*" Angels don't have the testimony of Jesus. They were created for a different time and purpose by God. So, this is not an angel John has encountered.

So, who is it? In my opinion, this being is part of a great cloud of witnesses and is on assignment to show John the mysteries of Heaven. You may be wondering, *We're not supposed to do that.* Well, the Bible says that a great cloud of witnesses is surrounding us. There is a really thin veil between the natural and the supernatural. When people die and go to Heaven, they are not on a cloud playing a harp somewhere. I believe they can be given assignments in Heaven. The Bible says there are souls underneath the altar crying out, *"How long, O Lord...until You judge and avenge our blood?"* (Rev. 6:10). People are still offering prayers in the courts of Heaven, in the counsel of Heaven.

The being John sees is not an angel; that means he is part of the cloud of witnesses. Why is that significant? Because he's so glorious that John wants to worship him.

> ## IF OUR VEIL OF FLESH IS HIDING THE GLORY THAT'S REALLY IN US AND IT WAS REMOVED, WE'D BE ABSOLUTELY SHOCKED AT WHO WE REALLY ARE!

The enemy wants to hide from us who we really are. In false humility, Christians claim, *Oh, I'm just a sinner saved by grace.* I'm not! I refuse to *just* be a sinner saved by grace. I'm the righteousness of God in Christ Jesus and I have a right to stand in the courts of Heaven and see verdicts rendered on behalf of nations—*you do too!* We are the righteousness of God in Christ Jesus. This being is literally the difference between how God sees us and how we see ourselves. This being in Revelation 19:10 is us, but without a veil of flesh to contain the glory that is resident within.

That's what Colossians 1:27 tells us, *"which is Christ in you, the hope of glory."* There's a glory in us. So why is this important? Because the anti-Christ spirit has two agendas. One, to deny and diminish who Jesus is. Two, to deny and diminish who we are in Jesus. Because if we ever figure out who we are in Jesus, we can change the world.

To operate with effectiveness in the courts of Heaven, you need to have a revelation of *who you are.* This only comes through prophetic revelation in the spirit realm!

## REFLECTION

Using the clear basis of Scripture, how does God see you? (Consider Colossians 1:27, Ephesians 2:6, and 2 Corinthians 5:21.)

_____

_____

_____

_____

_____

_____

_____

Why do you think you need a *prophetic understanding* to see the glory that is within you and understand your New Covenant identity?

Explain why you think the devil is so opposed to Christians stepping into an understanding of who they *really* are in the spirit realm—and operating out of this identity.

# THIRD DIMENSION OF PROPHETIC SIGHT: PARTICIPATION IN THE PROPHETIC REALM

*But you have come to Mount Zion, to the city of the living God, the heavenly Jerusalem. You have come to thousands upon thousands of angels in joyful assembly, to the church of the firstborn, whose names are written in heaven. You have come to God, the Judge of all, to the spirits of the righteous made perfect, to Jesus the mediator of a new covenant, and to the sprinkled blood that speaks a better word than the blood of Abel.*
—HEBREWS 12:22–24 NIV

In this passage, the writer is describing a spiritual realm that believers come to during their lifelong journey on earth. When he says you will come to Mount Zion, he's not talking about getting on a plane and flying to Israel and standing on Mount Zion outside the gate of Jerusalem. He's saying you have come to the heavenly Mount Zion—a spiritual dimension into which you have been given access through the blood of Jesus. You have already arrived at all these places.

Ephesians 2:6 says that *we are seated together with Him in heavenly places.* The places cited in Hebrews are an expansion of where we are seated. In other words, we are already seated with Him, right in the middle of all that we have come to. I keep telling the church we have a problem—we keep trying to get to places we've already come to. We've already been given a place in this realm; we are seated with Jesus in heavenly places. This is where we are, so if we come to this, it means we're part of it. We're not just spectators. We are participants.

Because we are there, it's reasonable to believe that there will be times when we encounter the activity that we are in the midst of—the blood speaking, Jesus the Mediator testifying, spirits of the righteous, the cloud of witnesses. Innumerable companies of angels guard the Church of all. This is the place where you operate in the court system of Heaven. The Bible says you have come to this place— even though your feet are on earth, in the spirit realm you are seated with Him in heavenly places right in the middle of all this supernatural activity. There will times when prophetically you will see and sense His activity so you can agree with it and see verdicts rendered out of the courts of Heaven.

All of a sudden, the prophetic is much bigger than what we thought. It's not just prophesying a simple word every now and then, as good as that can be. It's also discerning the activity that the Bible says we're right in the middle of. Maybe you never heard anything like what I'm teaching. That's because religion has said we shouldn't go there. *That's mystical.* Well, I'm sorry, but that's what the Bible says is available to you and I. The realm we've been functioning in has got us this far. But it hasn't taken us where we need to be yet.

If I can't see it and find it in Scripture, I'm not going there. I'm not going to tell you something I cannot prove biblically. This, however, is all clearly presented in the Bible.

So I invite you to join me in this prayer, asking the Lord to take you into this prophetic participation:

*Lord, would You by Your Spirit let me come into these realms?*

*Not just discerning what's in the books so I can present cases. Not just agreeing with the testimony of Jesus through the Spirit of prophecy.*

*Lord, I want to see and sense where I've come to.*

*I ask You to open my eyes to the spiritual realities I've been brought into, not just to give me an experience but to bring me into a greater understanding of the position You've called me to operate from.*

*I confess that I am seated by faith in this realm where the courts of Heaven operate, and I ask You to open my eyes to see and even experience some of these heavenly realities now so I can agree with Heaven and pull Heaven into the earth.*

*As I unlock my destiny and the destinies of others from the courts of Heaven, may this prayer be fulfilled:*

*Your Kingdom come,*

*Your will be done, on earth as it is in Heaven.*

# PRAYER TO STEP INTO THE PROPHETIC REALM OF THE COURTS OF HEAVEN

In previous sessions, you have confronted curses aimed at your destiny from being fulfilled. You've retrieved and opened your book of destiny. Now, I believe the Lord wants to help you see prophetically in a new dimension so that you can have clear access to what's written in your book of destiny and, also, what's written in the books of destiny for others.

As we finish this interactive course, allow me to ask the Lord to open the courts of Heaven so you can step in and look, feel, sense what is happening there. I offer the following prayer for you, dear reader:

> *Father, we thank You for loving us so much. Lord, I want to ask now that You would grant me entrance into the courts of Heaven. Lord, as I come and posture myself before You, I ask You to open, in the spirit realm, the doors of the court and allow me entrance before You. Thank You, Lord.*
>
> *I see the doors opening and I am standing before You, honoring You and loving You. As the doors have opened, I want to step into this dimension of the courts of Heaven.*
>
> *Lord, please allow me to look into the courts and encounter You and see the realms where You live and dwell, and even the places where You would allow me to function and that You say I have come to. I thank You for this, Lord.*
>
> *Thank You for Your presence, Lord.*
>
> *Thank You for opening the doors and opening the gates, Lord.*
>
> *Thank You, Jesus, for Your grace that abounds over me. Hallelujah!*
>
> *You are worthy, oh God.*
>
> *You are worthy of adoration.*
>
> *You are worthy of praise.*
>
> *I ask, Lord, that there be an activation in and from the courts of Heaven to be able to tread Your courts—that You would grant me entrance before You so I can understand how to come in and go out in the courts of Heaven and present my cases before You.*

# ABOUT ROBERT HENDERSON

ROBERT HENDERSON is a global apostolic leader who operates in revelation and impartation. His teaching empowers the body of Christ to see the hidden truths of Scripture clearly and apply them for breakthrough results. Driven by a mandate to disciple nations through writing and speaking, Robert travels extensively around the globe, teaching on the apostolic, the Kingdom of God, the "Seven Mountains," and most notably the Courts of Heaven. He has been married to Mary for over 38 years. They have six children and five grandchildren. Together they are enjoying life in beautiful Midlothian, Texas.

# FREE E-BOOKS?
## YES, PLEASE!

Get **FREE** and deeply-discounted **Christian books** for your **e-reader** delivered to your inbox **every week!**

## IT'S SIMPLE!

**VISIT** lovetoreadclub.com

**SUBSCRIBE** by entering your email address

**RECEIVE** free and discounted e-book offers and inspiring articles delivered to your inbox every week!

Unsubscribe at any time.

## SUBSCRIBE NOW!

LOVE TO READ CLUB

visit **LOVETOREADCLUB.COM** ▶